China's Reform and Opening Up and the Construction of Economic Development Zones

Edited by

Wang Jinding, He Lisheng and Zhao Quanmin

Published by
ACA Publishing Ltd.
University House
11-13 Lower Grosvenor Place,
London SW1W 0EX, UK
Tel: +44 (0)20 7834 7676 Fax: +44 (0)20 7973 0076
E-mail: info@alaincharlesasia.com

Web: www.alaincharlesasia.com
Beijing Office
Tel:+86(0)10 8472 1250 Fax:86(0)10 5885 0639
Written by Wang Jinding, He Lisheng, Zhao Quanmin
Edited by David Lammie
Translated by Xu Haiming
© People's Publishing House, 2015
This translation is published by ACA Publishing Ltd in association with People's Publishing House

ALL RIGHTS RESERVED. NO PART OF THIS
PUBLICATION MAY BE REPRODUCED IN MATERIAL FORM,
BY ANY MEANS, WHETHER GRAPHIC,
ELECTRONIC, MECHANICAL OR OTHER, INCLUDING
PHOTOCOPYING OR INFORMATION STORAGE, IN
WHOLE OR IN PART, AND MAY NOT BE USED TO PREPARE
OTHER PUBLICATIONS WITHOUT WRITTEN
PERMISSION FROM THE PUBLISHER.

The greatest care has been taken to ensure accuracy but the publisher can accept no responsibility for errors or omissions, or for any liability occasioned by relying on its content.
ISBN 978-1-910760-15-4
China's Reform and Opening Up and the Construction of Economic Development Zones is available from the National Bibliographic Service of the British Library.

Preface

What is the state system of China? How has the Communist Party of China (CPC) managed to exercize long-term governance and to lead the Chinese people from one victory to another? What are the 'secrets' of the CPC's governance? What is China's development road? What significant strategies have been adopted in China? What is the next step in China's development? Why has China been able to achieve such rapid economic development? These are just some of the many questions frequently asked by the international community, especially foreign political parties and statesmen on their visits to China. For the purpose of providing answers to these questions and enabling readers to be informed about the real China and the CPC, we arranged for the *Understanding Modern China* Series (hereinafter referred to as the Series) to be written, to serve as elementary documents introducing the CPC, as well as China's development road, development theories and development experience.

The Series is inspired by the new philosophies, new ideas and new strategies for the country's governance put forward by General Secretary Xi Jinping since the 18th National Congress of the CPC, aimed at the following aspects: strenuously reflecting the development vision of 'the Chinese Dream' and the development prospects of the 'Two Centenary' goals; strenuously reflecting the coordinated promotion of the overall situation of a 'five-pronged approach to building socialism with Chinese characteristics to build up socialist economy, socialist democracy, socialist advanced culture, socialist harmonious society and socialist ecological civilisation; and the strategic arrangements for the 'Four-Pronged Comprehensive Strategy' comprehensively completing the building of a moderately prosperous society in all respects, comprehensively deepening reform in all respects, comprehensively advancing the rule of law, and comprehensively exercising strict discipline for the party; strenuously reflecting the 'new normal' facilitating and leading China's economic development and the implementation of the 'five major development concepts' to promote innovative, coordinated, green, open and shared development; strenuously reflecting the three major economic development strategies of the 'Belt and Road', the coordinated development of Beijing, Tianjin and Hebei province, and the Yangtze river economic belt. On the basis of a great number of fresh cases and experiences, the Series tells China's story, transmits China's voice, analyzes China's problems, and offers China solutions.

The Series has been written on the basis of telling China's story and transmitting China's voice, oriented around the following four aspects: the first is to illustrate the new measures taken to deepen reform since the 18th National Congress of the CPC, the new ideas on economic development and the new philosophy on foreign affairs, on the basis of an all-round introduction to the achievements since the reform and opening up; the second is to analyze the reason for the achievements, the underlying operating law, and the process of evolution, while presenting the development achievements of China's economy and society; the third is to keep to problem orientation and demand orientation, rather than attempt to be all-embracing and systematic, so as to clear up targeted doubts and confusion on the basis of the demands of foreign readers; the fourth is to introduce China not only in terms of 'where it is coming from', but also in terms of 'where it is going', for the purpose of enabling readers to know about China's historical development process on the one hand, and on the other hand, exemplifying and clarifying how China assures the organic unification of its past, present and future, the organic combination of legacy and innovation, and how China is planning its future development.

Under the guidance of the International Department of the CPC Central Committee, the writing of the Series has been organized by China Executive Leadership Academy Pudong (CELAP).

The International Department of the CPC Central Committee is the functional department of the CPC in charge of foreign affairs. So far, the CPC has established connections of various types with more than 600 political parties and organizations in over 160 countries and regions, which include left-wing and right-wing parties; both ruling parties and opposition parties. Foreign affairs work is of paramount importance to the CPC, and an indispensable component of national diplomacy as a whole, whose target is to promote state-to-state and people-to-people communication and understanding.

Preface

CELAP is a national leadership institution in China, and as a platform on which international cooperative training and exchange are carried out, CELAP has held fast to its characteristics of internationality and openness since March 2005 when it was founded. CELAP spares no effort in implementing international cooperative training, with target participants being foreign political parties and statesmen, high-ranking business executives and senior professionals. By the end of 2015, CELAP had offered training programs to more than 6,000 participants from over 130 countries, and thus has won wide recognition and received a favorable reception from the countries, regions and participants that are involved.

To cater for the needs of foreign participants, CELAP initiated the writing of the Series at the beginning of 2012, and after four years of modifications and improvements, the finalized manuscripts were completed at the end of 2015. The first batch of 10 books to be published in this Series are: *China's New Strategies for Governing the Country; The Communist Party of China: the Past, Present and Future of Party Building; China's Reform, Opening Up and Construction of Development Zones; The Framework of the Chinese Government and Public Services; A New Analysis of Urbanization in China; China's Agriculture and Rural Development in the Post-Reform Era; The Evolution of China's Diplomacy in the Modern Era; Leadership Selection and Appointment in China; Leadership Education and Training in China;* and *Shanghai – the 'Pacesetter' of China's Reform and Opening Up.*

The authors of the Series are mainly professionals in CELAP, and functionaries and specialists in the Development Research Center of the Shanghai Municipal People's Government, Shanghai Institute for International Studies and Hangzhou Research Center for Urban Studies.

The Series is published in Chinese and English, with the English translation done mainly by senior professors at Shanghai International Studies University, to whom thanks are due. Gratitude also goes to the People's Publishing House for its great support and positive suggestions in the process of writing and translating.

Writing such a series of textbooks for mature foreign students is a first in China. Constructive criticism is welcome, for the Series as a new endeavor can hardly be free from mistakes.

Editorial Committee of the *Understanding Modern China* Series
January 2016

The Editorial Committee of the Understanding Modern China Series

Directors: Guo Yezhou Feng Jun

Vice Directors: Zhou Zhongfei   An Yuejun

Members: (Listed alphabetically)

An Yuejun	Chen Zhong	Feng Jun
Guo Yezhou	He Lisheng	Jiang Haishan
Li Man	Li Yanhui	Liu Genfa
Liu Jingbei	Wang Guoping	Wang Jinding
Yang Jiemian	Zhao Shiming	Zheng Jinzhou
Zhou Zhenhua	Zhou Zhongfei	

Editor-in-Chief: Feng Jun

Alain Charles Asia (ACA) Publishing Ltd is delighted to be associated with the People's Publishing House to bring this series of 10 *Understanding Modern China* books to an English-speaking readership.

ACA, formerly known as ACP (Alain Charles Publishing) Ltd Beijing, was founded in October 1989 and was the first foreign-owned publishing company to be allowed to open an office in China.

In 2007, ACP Beijing was renamed ACA Publishing Ltd to better reflect its focus on China and the Asia-Pacific region. The company specialises in publishing books about China for international readers and has offices in Beijing and London.

ACA Publishing Ltd,

April 2016

Contents

Introduction X
    0.1 Objectives XI
    0.2 Structure of the textbook XI
    0.3 Focal points and difficulties XIII
    0.4 Requirements XIII

1. Why Does China Need Reform and Opening Up? 1
    1.1 The highly centralized planned economic system 1
    1.2 Reform and opening up – a historical choice 5
    1.3 Economic and social conditions bring about
        reform and opening up 10

2. What are the Phases and Contents of China's
Reform and Opening Up? 12
    2.1 Major phases in reform and opening up 12
    2.2 Contents of reform and opening up 24

3. What are the Major Achievements of China's
Economic Reform? 44
    3.1 Continuous, steady and rapid economic growth 44
    3.2 Rapidly improving living standards 50
    3.3 Rapid development of the mixed ownership economy 54
    3.4 The shaping of a unified and open market with
        orderly competition 56

4. What are the Basic Practices of Deepening
Reform and Opening Up in China? 62
    4.1 Reform and opening up is a source of vigor for
        contemporary China to develop and progress 62
    4.2 Taking development as the key to solving all problems 68
    4.3 Stability is a precondition for reform and development 74

5. Why were Development Zones Designed as Part of Reform and Opening Up? 78
  5.1 The types and growth of development zones 78
  5.2 The practices and features of China's construction of development zones 80
  5.3 The achievements and experiences of development zones 87

6. What are the Features of Representative Development Zones in China? 93
  6.1 The construction and development of Shenzhen SEZ 93
  6.2 The construction and development of Pudong New District 107
  6.3 The construction and development of Suzhou Industrial Park ...113
  6.4 The practice and exploration of Kunshan ETDZ 120
  6.5 The construction of China (Shanghai) Pilot Free Trade Zone 126

Chapter Follow-up Questions and References 132

Introduction

China's reform and opening up, which was initiated in 1978, is, in essence, a reform of its former planned economy and an opening up of its closed economic system.

What, then, is the very source of China's reform and opening up, and what is its ultimate aim? It breaks with the old planned economy and aspires to the construction of a socialist market economy. This transformation from socialist planned economy to socialist market economy can be regarded as 'the greatest economic reform in its history'. Over time, it changed the property ownership system and altered the structure of resource distribution.

China's reform is moving ahead in parallel with the process of opening up. The two are, in fact, inextricably intertwined. Opening up facilitates reform, whereas the latter drives the former.

For more than three decades, China has determinedly pushed forward the reform of its economic, political, cultural, social and ecological systems, as well as the system of party construction. China has also aggressively intensified its economic interaction with other nations by relaxing, and even abolishing, many kinds of restrictive policies, attracting foreign investment and joining the international division of labor. In the face of ongoing economic globalization, China has adopted a comprehensive opening-up strategy. Both its reform and opening up can be seen as transformations that weed out the obsolete and stimulate the new. Both aspects are nothing short of uncommon explorations and experiments; both have made stunning global achievements.

Having passed through a planned economic system and having set in

Introduction

motion a socialist market economic system, China's reform is now entering a crucial phase that requires thorough reform, complete opening up and constant improvement of the socialist market economic system.

0.1 Teaching objectives

Taking the reform and opening-up process as well as the construction of economic development zones as its important background, this textbook analyzes and summarizes the practices, experiences and achievements of China's economic reform and opening up. In particular, it focuses on how the country has been marketizing its economy, advancing opening up and constructing development zones so that readers can acquire a better understanding of China's practices in these areas and of the differing modes of development, as well as of the theories behind those practices. Informative and enlightening, this book can help foreign readers relate China's experience to that of their own countries, with proper adjustment according to their specific local circumstances.

0.2 Structure of the textbook

This textbook contains six chapters. **Chapter one** analyses the historical background against which China's reform and opening up took place. Any social reform emerges from a prevailing crisis faced by society. Reform and opening up is then needed to help society overcome the crisis it is facing. Poverty is not a birthmark of socialism. The desire among the population for a good life and the pursuit of social progress constitute the fundamental motivations of reform. That is why China has already decided to end its highly centralized planned economy and is progressing toward a socialist market economy.

By taking the course of reform and opening up as its major theme, **chapter two** concentrates on China's transformation from a socialist planned economy to a socialist market economy in terms of its aims and selection of approaches. It also focuses on the construction and improvement of the socialist market system, and on the reform of the rural economic system, of urban state-owned enterprises, of the government administrative system and so on. These reforms, initially, 'fumbled their ways for stones as footholds across the river'. Nevertheless, they managed to move forward, step by step, and gradually deepened the reforming practices in the hope of finding the right direction and aims.

Finally, the third plenary session of the 18th central committee of the Communist Party of China (CPC) asserted that the general objective to reform more comprehensively is to improve and develop socialism with Chinese characteristics and to further modernize the country's governance system and improve its governing ability.

Chapter three selects as its main thread the achievements of China's reform and opening up, summarizing the benefits that have resulted over more than three decades. The benefits include economic growth, industrialization, urbanization, the establishment and improvement of a socialist market economy, constant perfection of the basic socialist economic system, the development of a mixed ownership economy, the raising of living standards and the perfection of the government macroeconomic management system.

Chapter four deals with China's reform, development and stability, by analyzing how the country has deftly handled these issues during the process of reform and opening up. In dealing with any kind of problem, China applies the following principles: reform serves as the impetus; development as the major task; and stability as the precondition. To properly coordinate reform, development and stability requires boldness, steady steps and a clear direction. China has found a path of development that, overall, suits its own national conditions, while at the same time achieving an internal coherence and balance of reform, development and stability.

The practicalities and explorations in the construction of development zones are dealt with in **chapter five**. This chapter introduces the types, features and practices of development zones. As is widely known, development zones have been integral in allowing China to develop its export-oriented economy. They have become engines that drive the regional economy. As 'pilot areas' and 'test areas' of reform and opening up, development zones have been highly innovative in terms of system and have constantly been used to reform the economic system in areas such as foreign investment, technology, management, imports and exports, and industrial restructuring.

Some highly representative development zones are cited in **chapter six** to highlight their orientations, practices, explorations and experiences. The repercussions are also discussed in greater detail in this chapter. The six development zones are Shenzhen (in Guangdong province), Pudong and China Pilot Free Trade Zone (in Shanghai), and Suzhou and Kunshan (in Jiangsu province).

0.3 Focal points and challenges

This textbook focuses on introducing China's practice of reform and opening up over the last 30-odd years, and on the experiences and lessons gleaned from the reform of its economic system. It aims to help readers understand how China, in the process of reform and opening up, made changes to its original rural economic system and state-owned enterprises; how it carefully evaluated and finally opted for particular strategies; what it considered and did while implementing the reform and opening-up schemes; how it successfully transformed itself from a highly centralized, planned economy into socialist market economy; how a relatively poor and backward country achieved rapid development; and how it rose from being the world's 10th largest economy in 1978 to the second largest one today. Its national economy, once on the verge of meltdown, is now a 'major engine' or 'stabilizer' that helps the global economy to function well. From rapid, extensive growth to intensive growth, from factory-driven to innovation-driven, China's economy has returned to a new normal state.

The challenges with this textbook include: how to meet the needs of foreign readers and how to arouse their interest; how to analyze the features and demands of cross-cultural communication; how to use simple, yet vivid language to recount China's reform and opening-up experience, how to graphically describe the process with typical examples, and how to supply practical and useful materials to foreign readers so that they can familiarize and identify themselves with China.

0.4 Requirements

Readers of this textbook should have acquired some understanding of the theories about China's reform and opening up. This book contains some basic information on the country's epoch-making undertaking. The reform and opening up of the country is a long, dynamic and evolving process, but the author is only able to analyze historical data covering a specific period, such as the market economy up to 2015. This makes analysis a static process since the events have already occurred and the information is stable. This requires teachers to constantly update their knowledge of the most recent reform progress and trends; to learn and acquire new knowledge on this front so as to be able to pique their students' interests. For students, while taking the textbook as their staple food, they are also expected to keep an eye on China's new reform drive to sharpen their understanding of the country's ongoing reform and opening up.

This book might contain shortcomings due to the limited knowledge of the writers and editors. Constructive comments are always appreciated.

A final note about the authors of this textbook: it is a joint venture between Wang Jinding, He Lisheng and Zhao Quanmin, with He Lisheng having overall control and the final say. The book may contain some errors and inconsistencies. Any critique and/or correction concerning this final version are equally appreciated.

Chapter 1

Why Does China Need Reform and Opening Up?

Social reform always grows out of a living crisis facing society. Reform and opening up is needed to get society out of this crisis. That is true in the case of China, where the long-established planned economy brought the country to the brink of collapse. It is why China began to set in motion the reform and opening-up process in 1978.

1.1 The highly centralized planned economic system

1.1.1 Characteristics of the planned economic system

A planned economy, or planned economic system, is a kind of economic system under which the state produces and allocates resources according to the fiat of the government or some financial groups. Nearly all planned economic systems rely on government mandates. It is for this reason that a planned economy is also called a 'mandatory economy'. China had been practicing a planned economy for nearly 30 years since 1950 when finance and the economy were centralized by the government. The impact was far-reaching. The establishment of this kind of economic system drew in large part on the economic mode and experience of the Soviet Union. True, the system proved to be instrumental in fixing the severe political and economic problems confronting the newly-founded People's Republic of China (PRC), at least for a time. Its characteristics were embodied in the following two aspects.

(1) **Public ownership dominated ownership structure.** From the perspective of ownership structure in China, it was quite obvious that, before the inception of reform, people's communes were large and highly socialized. According to the degree of socialization, urban industrial ownership fell into the following three categories: ownership by all the people; state ownership; and collective ownership. In rural areas, for instance, most of the land was

owned by the state or rural collectives. With no entire collective property rights, rural collectives had to strictly follow government orders to purchase and to produce. For example, national revenue in 1956 showed that the public sector accounted for as much as 90% of the economy; the percentage of individual sectors fell to 7.1%, while the private sector's contribution was less than 0.1%.

(2) The government directly regulated economic activities with mandatory orders. A centrally planned economy was marked by the fact that the state or the central government was largely responsible for running the economy, whereas enterprises, as government subsidiaries, only implemented their pre-determined production plans. The state regulated and controlled economic operations mainly through periodical economic plans. The state achieved all-round control through building special departments to map out economic development plans, setting targets or economic planning parameters for enterprises, and evaluating their performance that depended wholly on their fulfillment of the plans and preferences of the authorities. This planned or mandatory economy required detailed plans involving all the aspects of economic operation. For lack of information, the plans or schemes were often too rigid and inflexible. The reasons were as follows.

First, the power to make economic decisions was highly centralized. The state took charge of resource distribution on both the macro and micro front by planning revenues and expenditure, both for enterprises and individuals. This led to the reality that no actual microeconomic bodies other than the state and the government could exist. Such a system made economic decision-making highly centralized in the central and provincial head offices under the party's administration system; enterprises, individuals, legislative and judicial institutions and lower-level party administrative offices had no decision-making power. Later on, the power became even more centralized in the hands of a few leaders, whose personal principles and unprofessional decisions held sway over collective decisions. This inevitably resulted in a raft of wrong-headed decisions, severely disrupting the normal functioning of a planned economy.

Second, social resources were allocated according to existing plans. The core mechanism for planned resource distribution resided in it, replacing the price mechanism with administrative orders. In a centrally planned economic system, the role of the market in allocating resources through the price mechanism was downplayed as much as possible. Government plans and orders permeated every pore of the economy. Due to the rigidity of the orders issued about the flow of resources, allocation efficiency greatly decreased. As the bulk of resources were distributed according to the will of government, the structure of resource utilization became highly irrational. The authorities were prone to make resource distribution plans that, first and foremost, served political purposes instead of attending to the economic outcome. This was another important cause of the inefficiency of planned economic allocation.

Third, non-price features were used to index trading activities. Trading is the most common economic activity in human economic behavior. The core feature of a market economy lies in letting the price mechanism regulate trading, whereas in a planned economy trading activities are supplanted by administrative orders. The non-price feature of trading activity had its root in the mentality of the planned economy; it attempted to eliminate currency as the medium. This led people to seek alternative means, other than currency, to make payments, such as utilizing political power or taking a free ride. This is yet another factor that contributed to the low efficiency of the planned economy.

Fourth, in theory, income distribution should be made according to how much work one has accomplished. This requires a worker's gains to be determined by his/her contribution. Income distribution among socialist citizens follows the principle that 'the more you work the greater the benefits, the less you work the fewer the benefits and that you get nothing if you don't work and are not disabled'. But in China in that period, people worked together as collectives, and the production activities were carried out by cooperative social communities or teams, so it was impossible to accurately measure the output and contribution of individual workers. This made it difficult to put into practice the principle of making distribution according to the work one has actually done. In most cases, 'distribution according to work' finally turned into a kind of equalitarianism. Put another way, more labor did not guarantee more gain; nor did less labor necessarily mean less gain. Therefore, fewer people were willing to work harder and the number of free riders went up sharply.

The fifth reason is the polarization between the city and the countryside and its attendant dual structure. Out of strategic consideration, the planned economic system was adopted to catch up with developed countries, so considerable investment went into developing urban areas and heavy industry. However, as most newly-founded socialist countries were traditional agrarian states without abundant capital or large economic output, they all extracted money from agriculture to support industry so that heavy industry could develop as a priority. Government investment and resource allocation usually gave priority to urban development and heavy industry. Such a strategy brought about a very sorry state: urban development impeded the progress of rural areas and heavy industry restrained the growth of agriculture. Rural areas and agriculture were suppressed and suffocated because undue favor and preferential policies were given to cities and heavy industry. This caused a breakdown in the chain of industrial development at the later stage of economic development and was the primary reason why China's reform should originate from rural areas in the years to come.

Sixth, the economy was closed to outsiders. Socialist governments were born at a time when the world's proletarian revolution was at its high tide. Clashes between the two social systems – capitalism and socialism – had been evident even prior to the emergence of the planned economy despite the fact that the new socialist governments had all expressed their wish to conduct normal business with other countries including western ones, and had adopted the guideline 'self-reliance supplemented by foreign help'. Although socialist countries had business and trade contacts with the outside world at an early stage, they did so in most cases merely for political cooperation. Even at a later stage, chasms emerged within socialist camps that made the planned economic systems even more closed to, and isolated from, the outside world. Generally speaking, the scale of foreign trade under the planned economy before the reform was severely limited.

Finally, political campaigns and movements effectively superseded economic activities. The efficiency standard for economic activities was displaced by political sense and consciousness. For instance, microeconomic entities displayed more enthusiasm for political activities and this enthusiasm relied very heavily upon political mobilization and ideological propaganda. Thus, a special system took shape in which many political activities replaced economic ones. One of the risks with such politicization of economic life was that, once there was a crisis in belief or political cool-down or turbulence, the economy would slump; even a moral crisis might hit society hard.

1.1.2 An evaluation of the planned economic system

When the PRC was newly founded, the population was sure how to build a socialist economy. Initially, China merely chose the Soviet model. It adopted the Soviet's planned economy in terms of resource distribution;

chose its absolute state ownership and collective ownership in cities and towns and people's communal ownership in rural areas, as far as the means of production were concerned. It opted for seclusion concerning foreign relations; it prioritized national defense and heavy industries concerning nation building. Naturally, the ensuing outcomes were: low productivity; a dearth of motivation to innovate or advance technology on the part of science and technology workers and companies; slow progress of technology; a huge waste of investment and construction and a widening gap in economic and social development between China and other countries.

A specific historical reason motivated China to practice the planned economy. As we know, the planned economic system does have intrinsic advantages: first, it enables the government to participate directly in economic activities, to strengthen public sectors of the economy and accordingly, consolidate the newly established government; second, practicing a planned economy seems to be an effective way to stabilize the economy and to achieve industrial accumulation as fast as possible in a situation where, internally, economic life is in a mess and, externally, the country lags far behind western developed countries; third, the system seems to be very good at coordinating and solving all kinds of social problems that emerge from macroeconomic life and being able to allocate resources and to coordinate society. It seems to be good at maintaining a relatively high level of employment and at meeting people's most basic living needs. In short, the system suited our nation's economic conditions and the developing requirements at the earliest stage of socialist industrialization. The system also played a positive role during the earliest stage of China's socialist construction when the national economy was quite vulnerable; when its economic structure was so basic; and when the ruling party's prestige was very high and political enthusiasm was unprecedentedly heated. The drawbacks inherent in this system, however, began to become apparent all too clearly when the early-stage tasks of socialism were accomplished, when the expansion of the economy was continuing and when economic relationships grew more complicated.

1.2 Reform and opening up – a historical choice

1.2.1 Reform and opening up is a historical choice

As a new and grand undertaking spearheaded by the ruling party, reform and opening up does not happen by accident, but rather is deeply embedded in its historical background, internally and externally. On the one hand, given the nation's domestic situation, the 10-year-long Cultural Revolution had undeniably wreaked havoc upon the party, the country and its people, severely undermining the cause of socialism; on the other hand, in the light of the external situation, the new revolution of science and technology that took place across the world in the 1950s and 1960s actually stimulated the global economy. The gap between China and advanced countries in terms of the economy and technology had evidently widened. China was facing stiff competitive pressures. So the harsh conditions from within and the huge pressures from without forced China to choose reform and opening up. It was a forced, but also the only right option.

First, the decade of internal turmoil caused by the Cultural Revolution was a disaster for the party, the country and its people. The party's eighth National Congress drew a good roadmap for China to search for a new way to socialist construction, yet the Cultural Revolution from 1966 to 1976 was a massive and unprecedented calamity. Here's a description of China's economy and culture when the Cultural Revolution came to an end. Economically, the revolution caused a huge national economic loss. According to incomplete statistics, national income alone during the 10 years of revolution suffered a loss of Rmb500bn, equivalent to 80% of the total investment in infrastructure construction over the three decades since the founding of the state, and exceeding the total volume of the country's fixed assets over the same period. During the revolution, there was a period of five years when the economic growth rate was less than 4%. And in three out of the five years there was an economic downturn: -5.7% in 1967; -4.1% in 1968; and -1.6% in 1976. In February 1978, it was pointed out in *The Government Work Report* at the first session of the fifth National People's Congress (NPC) that, due to the havoc wrought by the Cultural Revolution, the whole country from 1974 to 1976 "lost Rmb100bn of industrial output value; 28m tons of steel output; and Rmb40bn of financial income, stumbling on the verge of collapse".

As for people's living conditions prior to reform and opening up, let us first take a look at urban residents. Most of them earned salaries. However, for about 20 years from 1957 to 1976, they enjoyed no pay raise. Their average salary was Rmb624 in 1957, which fell to Rmb575 in 1976, a decrease of Rmb49. Many consumer commodities were in short supply and had to be purchased with coupons. Grain coupons, in circulation for 40 years, were regarded as 'the second currency'. Although it only cost Rmb600 to buy all the five big commodities – a bicycle, watch, sewing machine, radio and camera – most families could not afford them even though they were greatly desired. Clothes were drab and dreary in both color and style, with blue, black, green and grey being dominant. At the beginning of reform and opening up, according to the national standard, roughly half of the 1.8m households in Shanghai – 899,800 of them – had housing problems. Three generations shared one room in 119,499 households; parents shared a room with teenage children in 316,079 households; sisters and brothers older than 12 shared a room in 85,603 households; 44,332 households shared a common room with another family; the average living space per person was less than two square meters for 268,650 households. Most houses comprised only bedrooms and kitchens, with no living room at all. A bathroom was usually shared by several households.

Now let us look at a farmer's life. According to the statistics compiled by the former People's Communes Committee under the Department of Agriculture, the average annual income the collective gave to each peasant was Rmb74.67 in 1978; 200m farmers earned less than Rmb50 a year. A total of 112m farmers each earned Rmb0.11 a day; 190m farmers earned Rmb0.13 a day; 270m farmers each earned Rmb0.14 a day. Quite a number of farmers, after a year of hard toil, earned no money at all. Instead, they would end up owing money to their production teams!

Second, the question 'What on earth does socialism mean?' took on an urgency in this period. The CPC had set socialism and communism as its objective since the day it was founded. Faced with the situation discussed above, people were bound to keep asking what was the advantage of socialism? Could socialism still attract, rally and unite the people if such a situation continued? Would the people agree? Is there any hope left for China? Anyone who cared about the future of the party and the country would pose such questions. On December 26, 1977, when meeting with the chairman of the Communist Party of Australia, Deng Xiaoping said: "Lenin frequently talked about the advantages of socialism. How can we show it? What is the advantage? Is it the advantage not to work or read? Is it the advantage that people's living conditions worsen instead of improve? If that is the 'advantage' of socialism, we had better give up."

At the first plenary meeting of the State Council on March 10, 1978, he said again: "What is socialism? In what sense is it better than capitalism? Each person, on average, has about 300kg of grain a year. Many people don't have enough to feed themselves. Only 23m tons of steel were produced over the past 28 years. Can that be called the advantage of socialism?"

When he was making inspections in the three north-eastern provinces in September 1978, he said: "Foreigners are discussing how long the Chinese can endure this. We should take note of their discussion. We need to ask how much we have done for the people… We are too poor, too backward. To be honest, we are unworthy of the people's trust… We shouldn't implement socialism in the present fashion if we want to see its advantage. Why do we need socialism if it was unable take us out of poverty after two decades?" These questions were actually a catalyst for people to rediscover what socialism really meant and how to construct it. We should by no means build socialism by carrying on with the Cultural Revolution. China could not in the least afford that revolution.

1.2.2 The rapid development of the economy and science and technology forces China to reform and open up

First, as the gap with other countries widened, China was facing tremendous pressure. From the mid-1950s to the mid-1970s, China launched the Great Leap Forward movement, the people's commune movement and the Cultural Revolution, in succession. Leftist blunders were made one after another. What were western countries, and the countries and regions around China doing at the same time? How were things over there?

A new revolution of science and technology was emerging. This revolution, also termed 'the third wave of scientific and technological revolution', started in the US after World War II. One significant characteristic of this revolution was that military technology, which was developed during the war to serve military purposes, was now being transferred to civilian use so that cutting-edge technology in the fields of atomic energy, information, biology and space developed rapidly and went into wide civil use. The US company Westinghouse Electric built the world's first commercial pressurized water reactor (PWR) nuclear power plant in 1957. The Soviet Union, the UK and France also built nuclear power plants. As nuclear power serves as a new source of energy, these power plants began to grow rapidly.

In the field of technology, the world's first ENIAC (electronic numerical integrator and computer) was created in the University of Pennsylvania in February 1946; a transistor computer came into being in 1958; in the second half of the 1960s, third-generation computers emerged that used integrated circuits and were capable of tens of millions of calculations per second; the world's first micro computer using a large-scale integration (LSI) chip was made in the US in 1971; as supercomputers were developing, microcomputers, microprocessors, home computers and personal computers were also making fast progress.

In the field of space technology, the Soviet Union successfully launched two man-made earth satellites on October 4 and November 3, 1957. Later, a heated space race began between the United States and the Soviet Union, which led to Apollo 11 becoming the first spacecraft to land on the moon in July 1969 and the space shuttle Columbia being launched successfully in April 1981. In the field of biotechnology, American scientists achieved the world's first successful DNA recombination in 1972; the world's first 'test tube baby' was born in Britain in 1978. New material technology and marine technology also developed rapidly. The new science and technology revolution transformed the world, its economic structure and people's modes of thinking, behavior and living having significantly propelled forward social productive forces.

Second, the main capitalist economies – the US, European countries and Japan – all achieved major economic progress. Powered by the new science and technology revolution, the US economy grew swiftly and continuously for 106 months from 1961 to 1969. The 1960s in the US was known as the 'prosperous decade'. Its GDP in 1971 reached US$1,526.5bn, 3.2 times that of 1957. Between 1951 and 1971, West Germany's GDP increased more than fivefold, the fastest growth rate among all western countries except Japan. From 1951 to 1970, France's industrial output grew by an average of 5.9% annually and its GDP shot up to US$140.9bn in 1970. Japan's development was particularly remarkable. Its *Five-year Plan for Economic Self-dependence (1956-1960)* was published in 1955, setting in motion an 'income-doubling program' that lasted for 10 years from 1960. Japan's economy grew by 8.5% annually on average from 1955 to 1960; by 9.8% from 1960 to 1965; and by 11.8% from 1965 to 1970. From 1955 to 1970, Japan's GDP increased 7.2 times. Rapid economic growth in Japan, the US and Europe continued until the outbreak of the oil crisis in 1973. This period was called the second 'golden era' for economic development in developed capitalist countries. During this period, China's neighboring countries and regions that used to be poverty-stricken, such as South Korea and Singapore, also achieved economic take-off. In the 1950s, South Korea's GDP was close to that of China's Shandong province. Yet, in the following 20 years, South Korea created what was known as the 'Han river miracle'. By the 1980s, it had totally eliminated poverty, with its GDP far ahead of that of Shandong.

Hong Kong's exports and imports totaled as much as US$19.6bn in 1977, compared with mainland China's US$14.8bn.

Third, the enormous gap stunned the world. It was through making trips abroad that people came to appreciate the wide gulf in science and technology between China and other counties. Since 1978, there was a rising wave of overseas inspection trips from China. Visitors at all levels who had been abroad shared a common feeling: it had never before occurred to them that modernization overseas should be so developed; that the gap between China and developed countries should be so huge; and that people's living conditions in western developed countries should be so much better than in China. With resentment and pain, people were acutely aware of the fact that China was too backward, and that it had been lagging behind for too long. If the CPC did not adjust its policies, seek another way out, reform and open up, and endeavor to catch up, it would fail to lead the people, the country and the era. On various different occasions, Deng Xiaoping talked about reform and opening. For example, in June and October 1978, when meeting guests from Romania and West Germany, he said: "We have sent many delegations to Europe and Japan for inspection. We see that there is a lot we can use; many counties are willing to offer us capital and technology with no harsh conditions attached. It is politically and economically beneficial to us, so why don't we do it?"

1.3 Economic and social conditions bring about reform and opening up

Seeing the huge gap between China and other countries, Deng Xiaoping pointed out: "Any delay to reform and open up would ruin the cause of our modernization and socialism." Later, the third plenary session of the 11th Central Committee of the CPC issued a communiqué, stating: "We should, based on the new conditions and experiences, take an array of significant economic measures to reform the economic management system and economic management methods. While adhering to self-reliance, we should also actively seek mutually beneficial economic cooperation with other countries on an equal basis and make use of the world's advanced technology and equipment." Although the phrase 'reform and opening up' did not appear in the communiqué, the above quote was clearly concerned with these matters. And so it was that China embarked on its grand task of reform and opening up.

Chapter 1

In short, over the 30-odd years between the founding of the new China and 1978, the CPC has been wishing to make the country a powerful and modernized state. To this end, it did indeed make considerable efforts and explorations. However, after the victory of revolution, the party failed to shift the focus of work from class struggle to economic construction. Seen from this perspective, the CPC's epoch-making decision to reform and open up should be counted neither as a historical coincidence nor as an individual's fantasy. Instead, it was an inevitable product, demanded by China's development, motivated by prevailing trends and driven by internal concerns and external pressures. To be sure, the choice was eventually made after a long and hard wrestle and struggle. In making the choice, China's communists again demonstrated their wisdom, courage and tenacity, for it is this choice that led China to achieving thorough and historic progress within the short space of 30 years. Just imagine if this decision was not made, or if another choice had been made to keep China still closed to the outside world, self-complacent and deeply mired in the leftist mindset, running against the tide of global development and people's fundamental and long-term interests; what would China be like now? What would Chinese society be like today? What would life be like for the billions of Chinese people? What would be the fate of the CPC, Chinese society and the Chinese nation? The answers are self-evident.

Chapter 2

What are the Phases and Contents of China's Reform and Opening Up?

2.1 Major phases in reform and opening up

China's reform and opening up refers to reforming internally and opening up externally. It is concerned with choosing roads to development and changing systems that govern the running of the economy. The practices, explorations and theoretical innovations made by the CPC's leadership which led the people in constructing socialism with Chinese characteristics are the manifestations of such grand reform.

2.1.1 Reform and opening up is mainly about the economic system

Mental emancipation heralded China's reform and opening up. It has allowed people to see things for what they are really are and to break any of their cognitive restrictions. It has helped to solve practical problems concerning the development of productive forces and the requirement that production relationships fit the development of productive forces.

Reform goes beyond economics, in which a highly centralized planned economic system has been transformed into a socialist market economic system. Reform is also aimed at political, social and cultural systems. For example, to develop democratic politics and to strengthen the rule of law is tantamount to a reform of the social and political systems, which aims to improve people's livelihoods and to achieve social harmony. First and foremost, however, economic reform constitutes the main content of reform and opening up.

First, reform ought to change the way in which resources are distributed by changing the distribution system; transform the highly centralized planned economic system into a market economic system; alter the planned system with highly concentrated power; change the resource distribution system in which resources are allocated according to administrative orders and arrangements; eradicate shortages in the supply of goods; build a market-oriented economic system in which the supply-demand relationship and price dictate resource allocation; and use the incentive and restrictive mechanism of market competition.

Second, reform ought to change the property organization system and nurture market participants. It has to clarify the relationships between the state and enterprises and give large-scale enterprises more rights to handle their own business. It has to propel state-owned and collective-owned enterprises to become independent entities that assume sole responsibility for profits and losses and to operate on their own, and into economic organizations whose power, responsibilities and interests are compatible with each other. Then the reform has to help these enterprises become independent legal corporate entities through ownership reform and the construction of a modern corporate system, and to help form a competitive market climate involving many kinds of economic sectors and entities by developing the private economy. Third, from where should the reform begin? How should it be implemented? Because of the complexities of the situation, there were too many aspects in need of reform. Thus, China was confronted with the following question: should it start from the economic system or the political system, or should comprehensive reform be launched?

In fact, reform started with the economic system, considering the reality that the centralized planned economic system had generated a rigid structure that was at odds with the development of social productive forces. The collective economy in rural areas didn't have a mechanism to incentivize or punish people. More labor or less labor, farmers received the same revenue. As a result, farmers found it hard to be motivated. Although 80% of China's population was engaged in agricultural production, grain output still fell far short of national demand. Enterprises in cities performed both governmental and corporate functions, and were artificially compartmentalized, ending up with low economic results. The government, however, controlled the enterprises too tightly, neglecting the role played by the market, commodity production and the law of value. Egalitarianism dictated distribution. Enterprises had no proper right to decide on issues affecting their own business, and therefore lacked verve and vitality. Neither the companies nor their employees had an abiding enthusiasm for production, to say nothing of technological innovation.

China's reform actually started in rural areas. Xiaogang village in Fengyang county, Anhui province began to practice the household contract responsibility system, signaling the beginning of China's reform of the economic system.

Reforms of state-owned enterprises and the planned economic system were the main focus of urban economic system reform. Opening up means removing red tape and getting connected with the outside world. China's opening up adopted a strategy of 'bringing in and going out', opening up the nation's door and market; connecting the domestic market with the global market, bringing in outside technology, investment and management; investing and doing business with foreigners; contacting other world economies; building special zones; joining the World Trade Organization (WTO); promoting exports and helping domestic enterprises to go global. Opening up is one of China's basic state policies, a way for the country to become strong, and a powerful driver for the development of societal affairs. In accordance with the special situations at different phases, China's reform and opening up set different goals for each phase and took different approaches, step by step, stage by stage and with varying focuses. Sometimes reform was pushed forward progressively through mandates; sometimes from top to bottom; at other times from bottom to top, or from both directions. To be effective and successful, reform needs to have different focuses while taking all aspects into consideration. The reform and opening up of a large country has to pass through different stages rather than be completed overnight. China's reform and opening up does not begin and end at a particular point in time. Instead, it has to last for a certain period. 'Rome was not built in a day'. One battle cannot win the whole war.

2.1.2 What stages has reform and opening up undergone?

The essence of China's reform and opening up is to liberate thinking, to emancipate and develop social productive forces, and to build socialism with Chinese characteristics. The general objective of furthering reform and opening up is to improve and develop socialism with Chinese characteristics and modernize the nation's administrative system and its capability. What stages, then, has reform and opening up undergone over the last 35 years? In accordance with the degree in which the market-oriented system was completed and the extent to which the socialist economy was constructed, China's reform and opening up has gone through the following stages.

The first stage was one of exploration – establishing a planned commodity economy based on public ownership. This stage spanned from 1978 to 1992, from the third plenary session of the 11th central committee of the CPC to the 14th National Congress of the CPC. By liberating thinking, seeking truth from facts and discussing practice as the sole standard for truth, this stage successfully shifted the focus from class struggle to economic construction, transformed the highly centralized planned economy to a planned commodity economy, and then completed the transition from planned commodity economy to early-stage socialist market economy.

The planned commodity economy was a type of socialist economic system in which the government plans and regulates commodity production, exchange and circulation based on public ownership of the means of production. The third plenary session of the 12th central committee of the CPC on October 20, 1984, pointed out for the first time: "The socialist economy is a 'planned commodity economy based on public ownership'." To develop a socialist planned commodity economy requires respect for the law of value both from the perspective of the government when making macroeconomic decisions and from enterprises when carrying out microeconomic activities. Gradually, government plans and the market will organically work in concert to form a regulatory mode to adjust economic operation.

Here are the main features of this phase. First, in terms of the economic operating system, plans and market cooperated under regulation, with plans comprising the main part and the market the remainder. The market regulated the newly formed commodity market. The markets of capital, technique and land had not yet come into being. Wherever important goods and resources that would affect national welfare and people's livelihood were concerned, government plans were needed. Second, in terms of the property organization system, the public-owned economy, including state-owned and collective-owned economies, dominated while the non-public economy served as a supplement. Enterprises were mostly owned by the state or collectives. There were self-employed household businesses but only a few enterprises were owned by private individuals. State-owned enterprises generally began to adopt the responsibility system in business operation and made attempts at the shareholding system. Third, government control over enterprises gradually became indirect; economic, legal and administrative means worked together to regulate the market supply-demand relation. And fourth, with opening up getting wider and deeper, special economic zones began to take shape, along with open coastal cities and coastal economic development zones.

The third plenary session of the 11th congress of the CPC, solemnly held in Beijing from December 18-22, 1978 (Xinhua News Agency)

The second feature was the phase of constructing a socialist market economy through the practice of reform and opening up, which lasted from 1992 to 2003. If 1978 marked the first year of China's reform and opening up, then 1992 was the first year when China embarked on the construction of the market economy. In the spring of 1992, Deng Xiaoping, chief architect of reform and opening up, inspected Shenzhen, Zhuhai and Shanghai, and during the journey made a series of significant speeches that were later known as his 'southern tour speeches'. Through these speeches, he vented the view that both the market and plans were economic means; capitalism also had plans; and socialism also had the market; plans and the market were not fundamental differences that distinguish socialism from capitalism. He proposed to construct a socialist market economy. In October 1992, the reports of the 14th National Congress of the CPC nailed down the construction of a socialist market economy as the objective of China's reform. A socialist market economic system was connected to the basic system of socialism. To build a socialist market economy, the market must be allowed to play a fundamental role in allocating resources under the government's macro regulation.

The main characteristics of this stage were as follows. The market played a fundamental role in resource allocation, as opposed to the supplementary role that it used to perform. More economic areas were subject to market regulation. Government control over prices was relaxed and replaced by the market system. Markets of productive factors such as labor, technique and capital took rough shape. The basic economic system took the public sectors of the economy as its bulk, meanwhile allowing economies of diverse

Chapter 2

ownership to co-develop, and actively developed non-public sectors of the economy while ensuring the dominant position of public ownership, because all kinds of non-public economy such as the self-employed household economy and private economy were also crucial to the growth of a socialist market economy. State-owned enterprises made further changes to their operating mechanism, adopting a modern corporate system that was to meet the requirements of the market economy and that was to be exemplified by clearly-defined property rights, power and responsibilities, separation of corporate functions from governmental duties and scientific management. Thus, governmental planning, fiscal policies and monetary policies ran in union and constituted the macro-regulatory system, which was still under constant improvement and acted as an economic leverage. The state furthered reform and opening up, joined the WTO, and maintained economic growth at a high rate, thereby greatly augmenting its comprehensive national power and accelerating its industrialization process.

The solemn opening ceremony of the 14th National Congress of the CPC, held in the Great Hall of the People, Beijing, on October 12, 1992 (Xinhua News Agency)

The third characteristic is the phase of improving the socialist market economic system. The main objective in this stage was to perfect the socialist market economic system. To this end, the relationship between government and market, a crucial and long-standing conundrum, must be handled well by respecting the law of the market and allowing the government to play its due role. In October 2003, the third plenary session of the 16th central committee of the CPC made it clear that reform of the socialist market economy should be furthered, with the purpose of perfecting the socialist market economic system. In November 2012, the 18th National Congress of the CPC proposed again that the work of improving the socialist market economic system should be expedited. In November 2013, the third plenary session of the 18th central committee of the CPC yet again proposed that deepening reform of the economic system should evolve around letting the market play a decisive role in resource distribution; that to further reform comprehensively, we should understand that the focus was on reform of the economic system; and that the core problem was to handle properly the relationship between government and market by allowing the market to determine resource allocation and for the government to improve its function where necessary.

The striking feature of this phase was that this mixed economy was developing in a stable and steady fashion. The basic economic system, in which the economy of public ownership serves as the leading force while the economy of other multiple ownerships co-develops simultaneously, constitutes the foundation of the socialist market economic system. Public and non-public ownership economies are both indispensable parts of China's socialist market economy. The property rights of the public economy can't be infringed upon; neither can those of the non-public economy. The government protects the property rights and legitimate interests of all economic sectors, regardless of ownership. The government ensures that all sectors of the economy shall have equal access to production factors according to the law; can participate in market competition openly, equally and fairly; and shall be well protected and strictly supervised by law. The government endeavors to construct a unified and open market system with orderly competition, and to quickly form a modern market system under which enterprises operate on their own and compete on a level playing field; consumers can choose and consume of their own will; commodities and factors circulate freely and are exchanged on an equal basis. The government makes fair, open and transparent market rules, reforms the market supervision system by unifying it, and eliminates all rules and practices that hamper fair competition and unification of the markets across the whole nation. The government bans illegal preferential policies, punishes those who make them, and cracks down on regional protectionism, monopoly and crooked competition. The government strives to perfect the mechanism within which the price should be determined mainly by the market. Wherever a price can work well in the market, then the role of the market has been given full play. The government also tries to develop and improve the markets of capital, technique and land. Although China has been reforming and opening up for 35 years and has become the world's second biggest economy, its 'market economy status' has not been recognized officially by developed countries, such as the US and EU members. China needs to continually further its reform of the economic system; to perfect its socialist market economic system more rapidly by letting the market decide on resource allocation and the government function better. It's a general rule of the market economy that the market decides how to allocate resources. To this end, the socialist market economic system must follow this rule by endeavoring to improve the market system, preventing the government from over-interfering and requiring the government to exert proper supervision. It is necessary to actively and steadily push forward marketization in breadth and depth; to greatly reduce the government's direct participation in resource allocation; and to allocate resources according to market rules, price and competition so as to maximize the benefits and optimize efficiency. This requires dealing with the relationship between government and market in a proper way. But how shall we deal with it?

First, the government needs to pass power over to the market and to accept its role as a disinterested supervisor. The 'visible hand' has to be less visible. The market needs to be respected and the 'invisible hand' should be felt more. The hand of the government should not replace the hand of the market. We should adhere to furthering marketization, actually perfect the market system mechanism, let the market play its basic role in optimizing factors and allocating resources, open up the market further, rely more on the market mechanism and remove administrative monopoly. Second, the pricing mechanism of resources should be forged and a market culture that honors the spirit of contract, honesty and equality should be built; we should protect intellectual property, encourage innovation and encourage the marketization of labor, land, capital and technique. Third, the main responsibility and function of the government is to stabilize the macro economy, strengthen and optimize public services, ensure the fairness of competition, reinforce market supervision, maintain market order, promote sustainable development, work for common prosperity and remedy market failures. To perfect the socialist market economy more rapidly requires taking scientific development as the theme and quickening the transformation of development models as the main thread. In order to improve and develop the economy, we must adjust the economic structure and widen the benefits of economic development. It's also the objective for the new development model. The requirement is focused on stimulating the vitality of all kinds of market players, driving innovation and development, constructing a new system of modern industrial development and cultivating a more favorable climate for developing an open economy.

The fourth phase is a new normal state that China's economy has recently entered. The economic new normal refers to a new phase of China's economic development containing new features. It means that China's economy is evolving into a new period where its form is more advanced, the division of labor is more complicated and its structure more rational.

Economic development has entered a new normal. The fast pace of development is slowing down a little. The development model is changing from extensive growth characterized by large scale and high speed into intensive growth characterized by good quality and high productivity. The driving force of the economy is shifting from traditional growth points to new ones. According to a detailed study, China's new normal possesses the following features. In terms of development speed, rapid growth has turned into a moderately rapid growth that is more rational. In terms of economic development model, more attention is paid to quality and efficiency, i.e. intensive growth. In terms of economic driving force, there is less reliance on factors and investment, and more on human capital, intangible assets and innovation. In terms of economic structure, instead of blindly expanding economic capacity, production capacity is adjusted according to market demand and technological advancement; the economic structure is being upgraded; consumer demand for the tertiary sector is gradually becoming mainstream; the gap between urban and rural areas is shrinking; people's incomes are increasing; the fruits born out of development are benefiting more people. China is now in the middle of late-stage industrialization. Industrial growth has stabilized at a slightly reduced level. The growth of the tertiary industry is accelerating. The industrial structure and connections between industries are becoming more sophisticated. More economic added value is created. Traditional industry should be upgraded and transformed and different infrastructure elements should be interconnected. New technology, products, business styles and business models are springing up, creating more investment opportunities. In terms of resource distribution and macro regulation, the government should function better and allow the market mechanism to play a decisive role. In terms of consumer demand, the stage of wave-shaped consumption style is nearing an end; personalized and diversified consumption has become the mainstream; the roles played by new industry, service industry and new business models have become more salient; miniaturization, intellectualization and professionalization of production may become new characteristics of industrialization; economic growth needs to depend more on human capital, technological progress and innovation as the new engines; economic development has to choose a green, low-carbon and cyclical approach.

2.1.3 What are the driving forces to continue and deepen reform and opening up?

First, continuing reform and opening up is the source of vigor for development and progress. China's reform and opening up has never halted but kept deepening over the last 35 years. In 1978, reform and opening up was proposed at the third plenary session of the 11th central committee of the CPC. In the 1990s, reform and opening up was confronted with a choice of direction. Deng Xiaoping's 'southern tour speeches' and the 14th National Congress of the CPC both pointed to constructing a socialist market economy. The subsequent third plenary session of the 16th central committee of the CPC proposed the perfection of the socialist market economy. In 2012, the 18th National Congress of the CPC proposed again to perfect the socialist market economy more rapidly. The third plenary session of the 18th central committee of the CPC proposed that reform of the economic system should be crucial to the comprehensive deepening of reform and opening up, and that the key should be to cope well with the relationship between the government and the market, letting the market play a decisive role in resource allocation and the government to function better. It's a general rule that the market determines resource allocation. To make the socialist market economic system sound, this rule must be followed, and problems relating to the imperfections of the market system must be tackled; that the government interferes too much and that government supervision is insufficient. After some 30 years of hard exploration, we have gained considerable experience and learned many lessons. From 'construction' to 'perfection', a thematic shift, we have achieved profound knowledge of the rules governing socialist economic construction. Significant thoughts, such as the 'Three Favorables', 'Three Represents', putting people first, a comprehensive, harmonious and sustainable development outlook, all-round development of the economy, society and people and the Chinese Dream, have enriched and developed the theories on the socialist market economy and the theories of socialism with Chinese characteristics.

As reform and opening up deepens and now stands at the crucial period of 'conquering fortresses' (facing some hard-to-solve but unavoidable issues), what can be relied on to rally the people, stimulate innovation and vitality, keep the economy growing and win comparative advantages? We rely on continuing reform and opening up because reform is still the banner with the greatest attraction. With the present system under transformation, innovation is still inadequate, and economic and social development is neither sufficiently harmonious nor well balanced. Problems such as urban-rural division, social stratification and restricted upward mobility, unfair distribution of income and severe corruption necessitate unremitting reform and opening up. There is no end to the process of reform and opening up. To stop or to hold back would lead to a dead end. We should continue to reform and open up, and stick to the road of socialist market economic reform. We should always try to promote social fairness and justice and bring people happiness. We should further liberate the mind, develop social productive forces and enhance social vitality. We should bring into full play all kinds of labor, knowledge, technique, management and capital; let all sources of social wealth flow abundantly and let all the fruits borne by reform and opening up multiply and benefit people equally. Thanks to reform and opening up, China is now closer to realizing the great rejuvenation of the nation than at any point in its history. To achieve this grand objective, China has found the socialist road with Chinese characteristics that suits national conditions.

Second, marketization, legalization and democratization are the basic trends of China's economic system reform. The objective of economic system reform is to build a socialist market economy that is vigorous, innovative, inclusive, orderly and safeguarded by the law. These specific measures are perfecting the market system, transforming government functions and innovating the enterprise system. The three measures comprise the 'trinity reform'. At its 12th National Congress, the CPC proposed to 'let the planned economy dominate and let market regulation act as a supplement'. At its 13th National Congress, the CPC proposed that the socialist planned economic system should be a system in which planning and the market coexist in concord. From the 12th to the 13th National Congress, the market-orientated outline loomed large and clear. The 14th National Congress of the CPC required that the aim of economic system reform should be to construct a socialist market economic system. The 16th National Congress proposed to finish constructing a perfect socialist market economic system by 2020. The 18th National Congress proposed to accelerate the perfecting of the socialist market economic system. The third plenary session of the 18th central committee of the CPC in November 2013 made it clearer that reform of the economic system was crucial to the comprehensive deepening of reform and opening up, and that we should bring into full play the 'towing effect' of economic system reform. It also proposed that we should focus on letting the market play 'a decisive role' in resource allocation while deepening economic system reform. The practice of reform has furthered our understanding of the market economy; the functions of the market have boosted our confidence in carrying ahead with reform in a determined manner.

Third, reform and opening up gathers steam for China's economy to continuously develop. The purpose for us in deepening reform and opening up is to fully unleash the pent-up innovative energy of the people and society, and stimulate the market's inherent momentum. To go deeper, we should take reform and opening up as the basic policy of development. We should remove control over the market, the 'invisible hand', and use government as the 'visible hand' in a positive manner. This way, we will be able to propel the economy steadily. To encourage social investment, we should further reform the investment, fiscal and financial systems, focus on developing the factors of production, stimulate more insightful ideas on the reform of investment and the financing system, and encourage and direct private capital to go more rapidly into all aspects of the economy, infrastructure construction, and social and public utility areas. We should reform government institutions and the project assessment and approval system in order to create a friendly climate for all market players to make investments and start businesses. We should help enterprises to have more productive energy. We should transform the government's responsibilities and functions into a body that provides public services. We should draw up a list of indsutries in which foreign investment is forbidden or restricted and adopt the national treatment principle, creating a fair, open, free and competitive market and business environment. We should adhere to the equality of rights, of opportunities and rules, pursue policies to reduce taxes, take substantial measures to support small businesses, and reduce operating costs for enterprises to help them grow. Reform and opening up brings 'dividends' and unleashes the development vigor of urbanization.

We should implement a new type of urbanization, optimize urban planning and layout, build a mechanism to balance public resource distribution between urban and rural areas, handle properly the relation of industrial development and urban construction, create an urban environment suitable for living and working, accelerate the reform of the household registration system, and give migrant workers the official identity as urban residents. Continuous reform and opening up is the greatest force powering the continuous growth of China's economy. History has clearly revealed this to be the case. First, rural reform heralded by the household contract responsibility system in the 1980s facilitated rural and agricultural economic development. Second, in the 1990s, the construction of the socialist market economic system and the reform of state-owned enterprises (SOEs), together with the rapid development of the non-public economy, boosted the urban economy. Third, with China officially acceding to the WTO in 2001, the domestic market has been connected to the global market and has participated in world market competition, so that China's manufacturing industry has become global and has benefited from economic globalization. Fourth, the third plenary session of the 18th central committee of the CPC in 2013 proposed to deepen reform comprehensively and set as a goal perfecting and developing socialism with Chinese characteristics and further modernizing the governmental administration system and administrative ability. To accomplish that goal, more attention should be directed to a systemic, holistic and well-coordinated reform and we should quickly develop the socialist market economy, democracy, advanced culture, harmonious society and conservation culture.

2.2 Contents of reform and opening up

The socialist market economic system is both a great invention of the CPC and the very source of vigor for China's economic and social development. Where the economic system is concerned, the road traveled by reform and opening up over the last 30 years has mostly involved transforming a highly centralized planned economy into a socialist market economy as well as constantly perfecting this market system. By using the supply-demand leverage, the price and competition mechanism, the market economy most efficiently and effectively allocates rare resources such as labor, capital, technique and other productive factors to different fields of production so that diverse demands can be met very quickly and economic efficiency can be augmented and wealth greatly increased.

2.2.1 Replacing planning with the market and giving the market a decisive role in allocating resources

Reform started from the market, for China badly needs a market economy. Its consumer market has fully developed while the factor markets of capital, land, technique and so on still require improvement. The mechanism of the market plays a decisive role in resource distribution.

First, we should build a unified, open and orderly competitive market system and ensure as soon as possible that in this market system enterprises operate on their own and compete fairly; consumers choose what to purchase of their own free will; commodities and factors flow freely and exchange hands on the basis of equality.

To begin with, we should reform the circulation system and cultivate rural markets. The major measures we should take are as follows.

First, we should reform the commodity circulation and wholesale systems to reduce the number of steps involved in circulation, and relax price controls; we should build a new and open circulation system where there are different kinds of economic sectors, circulation channels, business operation patterns, and fewer intermediate linkages. In the early stage of rural reform, grain was purchased mainly by the government. Because the closed market was unable to absorb the fast-expanding agricultural output, farmers had difficulty in selling grain or cotton. They had to queue to sell their products and so they were discouraged from producing more. After the relaxation of price controls, demand in the market led to a change in rural production structure so that it would cater to the diversified market demands. This overcame the difficulty in selling and earned higher prices for agricultural products.

In the mid-1980s, the central government encouraged farmers to develop township enterprises. As fast-developing township enterprises provided more and more products to the market, the structure of the national economy began to change. The booming township enterprises accounted for half of the national economy. With the rise of township enterprises, the rural population, products, information and capital began to flow in a way that they had never done before. The skills of the population were improved. The social classes were also undergoing a subtle change. As township enterprises prospered, the government relaxed its control over population mobility and allowed farmers to migrate to work in cities. This further broke the barrier of employment between urban and rural areas.

Then, we should reduce or even rescind administrative mandatory plans, nourish and develop commodity markets. We should expedite the formation of a modern market system where enterprises operate on their own and compete on a level playing field; where consumers choose what to buy of their own accord and where commodities and factors flow freely and are exchanged on an equal basis. We should remove market hurdles and improve the efficiency and fairness of resource allocation. We should first reduce or even revoke administrative planning, let the market regulate, reduce mandatory plans that control the number of commodities in areas of production and circulation; simplify red tape concerning project approval and elevate the government's ability to regulate the macroeconomy.

The measures in question that have already been taken are as follows.

First, we have relaxed government control over the types and numbers of commodity in the field of production and implemented price reform. In 1986, when the planned economy was being transformed into a commodity economy, in order to stabilize the market and stop prices from rising as a result of supply shortages, we began to make dual prices for consumption goods and production goods. As it happened, one kind of material or commodity had two prices so that the price wouldn't rise too fast. In 1987, in the field of production, governmental mandatory plans only covered 60 types of industrial product.

Second, we relaxed government control over the types and number of commodity in the field of circulation. For a time, the government planned or controlled all goods in circulation. In 1987, the government only controlled 23 types of goods. The stipulation about removing price controls required that controls over the price of more than 90% of consumer and production goods should be removed by the early 1990s, and that the market should be allowed to determine the price, so that the distortion of the pricing of many commodities and resources was erased and market barriers were removed for smooth commodity exchange and enterprise operation. Third, we actively cultivated the factor and capital markets. In 1991, China established stock exchanges in Shanghai and Shenzhen. China facilitated the reform of SOEs through actively developing the capital market. In 2005, China's NPC passed the revised *Securities Law* and *Company Law*. In 1992, the third plenary session of the 14th central committee of the CPC proposed clearly that SOEs should take the establishment of the modern enterprise system as their goal, adopt the corporate system, widen their ownership to include more types of non-state investor so that they become real market participants, and reform their organization and management systems. While reforming SOEs, we adjusted the structure of the state-owned economy so that it should lead the development of the national economy and provide basic products in crucial areas such as resources, finance and infrastructure sectors including transportation and communication. New research conducted in 2005 and funded by the Office of Fair Trading of China's Ministry of Commerce showed that the degree of marketization of China's economy was 73.8% in 2003, which was above the threshold level of 60%. Statistics since 2004 revealed that more than 95% of total retail sales of consumer goods were regulated by the market, as were more than 91.9% of the total sales of production goods. At present, wherever the market can decide a price, the market is given the entire right to decide, with no improper interference from the government. The government is now pushing for price reform in the areas of water, oil, gas, electricity, transportation and telecoms, introducing competition to adjust the price. Those fields where the government decides the price are confined to important public utilities, charity services and network-type natural monopoly sectors. The government increases the transparency of its regulation and accepts the supervision of society. We have also perfected the price mechanism of agricultural products and accentuated the role of the market in pricing.

Third, we should develop factor markets and perfect the market system. The modern system of a market economy requires not only developing the consumer market and the market of production goods; more important, it requires cultivating and developing factor markets of land, labor, capital, technology and so on. Since the 1990s, China has been breaking administrative monopoly and regional protectionism, pushing forward the development of commodities, and facilitating the reform of factor markets.

The major measures to realize these goals are as follows.

First, the labor market was maturing. In the late 1990s, employees of urban state-owned and collective-owned enterprises, with the breaking of their 'iron rice bowls' (meaning everything was guaranteed if you worked in the public sector or SOEs), entered the labor market. In the same period, college graduates who had to find a job for themselves also entered the labor market. After 2000, more than 200m peasant-workers came into the urban labor market. All these developments prompted the formation and gradual maturing of the labor market and helped to liberate China's labor force and significantly improve productivity. China's economic miracle is closely related to the adequate supply and high efficiency of the labor market.

Second, the capital market was established and developed. At the beginning of the reform, banks began to make loans to SOEs, instead of allocating them funds. In the early 1990s, shares were issued and the stock market emerged. Then state-owned financial institutions began to adopt the shareholding system. The establishment of financial institutions with various kinds of ownership (including foreign ownership) was permitted. The government built regulatory agencies to supervise banks, securities firms and insurance companies. All these indicated that the capital market was taking shape in China, but it was not yet fully or soundly developed. So it was necessary to introduce competition in order to further the marketization of the price of resources such as water, oil, natural gas, electricity, transportation and communication. Those fields where the government once decided the price were limited to important public utilities, charity services and network-type natural monopoly sectors. The government increased the transparency of its regulation and accepted the supervision of society. We accelerated the marketization of capital and perfected the mechanism that guides the marketization of the renminbi interest rate and exchange rate.

Specifically, we pushed the marketization of interest rates, eliminated the floor on lending rates and the ceiling on deposit rates; marketized the benchmark deposit rates and eased market access. We permitted capable private capital to start small financial institutions such as banks according to the law and perfected the mechanism for financial institutions to enter into, or retreat from, marketization. We established the deposit insurance system, perfected the multi-level capital market system, adopted the registration system concerning share issuance, developed a bond market, increased the ratio of direct financing, and hastened the realization of the renminbi's convertibility under capital accounts.

Third, the technology market has taken shape. We are building and perfecting the market-oriented system for technological innovation, giving free rein to the market and allowing it to play a guiding role in pricing technological research and development products and in allocating innovation elements. We are developing the technology market, perfecting the mechanism for technology transfer, improving conditions for small and medium-sized tech firms to finance, perfecting the system of venture capital, innovating business models, and facilitating scientific and technological achievements to achieve capitalization and industrialization. The marketization of technology remains insufficient and the scale is still limited, which has dented its competitiveness, especially in terms of sustainable competitiveness.

Fourth, a land market is beginning to take shape. Starting from nothing, the land market has taken off. Based on the fact that land ownership and usufruct are separated and that those farmers who have the right to use land lack the negotiation status they deserve in land transactions, governments at different levels still hold absolute control over land transactions in the primary market. The land market is still in formation, and the efficiency of land allocation remains low. The 18th National Congress of the CPC and the third plenary session of the 18th central committee of the CPC required the building of an integrated construction land market covering both urban and suburban areas. As long as it does not go against planning or land-use control, rural collective construction land for business purposes is allowed to be sold, leased or pooled as shares. It shares the same rights and price as state-owned land once it goes into the market. We have stuck with the collective ownership of rural land, safeguarding farmers' contract rights and relaxing control over management rights. Currently, we are accelerating the construction of a land exchange market and property rights exchange market, along with reform of the fiscal system. We are perfecting the system under which the financial capability and power of the central and local governments are in proportion. We are perfecting the public finance system that facilitates the equalization of public services and the construction of major function-oriented zones. We are building local tax systems to make the tax system beneficial to structure optimization and social fairness. We are building a system where public services can be sold and the earnings derived can be shared reasonably by the people.

2.2.2 The basic economic system with public ownership dominating in tandem with diversified ownership

First, we initiated rural reform and implemented the household contract responsibility system. Rural areas, farmers and agriculture all benefited the least, yet were also least controlled under the planned economic system. So, rural reform was comparatively easy to effect. This was the reason for initiating rural reform. Prior to the reform, the proportion of household income spent on food (known as the Engel coefficient) among rural families was 67%. Among the 700m rural people, 250m were in absolute poverty. Farmers had such difficulty in simply eking out a living that their desire to effect change and live better became the driving force of reform. For example, Xiaogang village in Fengyang county, Anhui province, the cradle of rural reform, used to be a well-known impoverished village whose people had to buy grain to feed themselves, and who relied on relief when money fell short and depended on loans to engage in production. In 1978, farmers from 18 households in Xiaogang, with extraordinary courage and insight, signed a contract with their blooded finger-prints (they were mostly illiterate and had no seals of their own) that started the rural contract responsibility system, ushering in the beginning of China's rural reform. Perhaps coincidentally, just as the farmers were signing with their finger prints, the third plenary session of the 11th central committee of the CPC was starting at the same time. Politicians represented by Deng Xiaoping, together with farmers at the lowest layer of economic society, turned a new page of history, shifting the focus of the party's work to the modernization of socialism. Later on, a set of policies was passed, permitting farmers, under unified government planning and guidance, to manage their land of their own free will and in accordance with the specific time and conditions so that farmers' enthusiasm in production could be encouraged and protected.

In 1980, the state issued a document entitled *Some Issues with Further Strengthening and Perfecting the Agricultural Production Responsibility System*, affirming the socialist nature of the practice of fixing a farm output quota for each household. Instituting the household contract responsibility system was actually a reform of the land system (property rights), making farmers their own masters in production and management. The land was owned by collectives, but farmers had the rights to use and manage it. Profits were divided among the state, the collectives and farmers. Through the land contract, the means of allocation was reformed. While providing grain and other farm products to the state and collectives, farmers could keep for themselves all that was left. In 1983, the household contract responsibility system was extended nationwide. This system and farmers' new status as their own masters in production and management guaranteed farmers' autonomy and laid a solid foundation for the construction of a rural market economy. Household contract management gave farmers a high degree of autonomy, allowing them to produce according to market demands and to choose to work in their preferred professions. This fully animated farmers' enthusiasm and greatly boosted the development of agriculture and the rural economy. The household contract responsibility system connected rural workers with the land. In the past, farmers ate together and earned the same income, regardless of their different labor contribution; farmers' interests were not directly related to production so they had no incentive in producing more grain. After the implementation of the household contract responsibility system, things were drastically changed. Farmers signed land contracts and took charge of production. As long as they gave the fixed quotas of farm products to the state and collectives, as required, they could keep the remainder for themselves. The reform organically combined the rights, responsibilities and interests of farmers, enhanced their enthusiasm for production and expedited higher yields. Farmers were permitted to migrate to cities and to freely engage in other trades. They could buy and sell agricultural products and other kinds of goods there. Urban markets were open to them. Urban-rural exchange became a reality. All this had promoted the growth of the rural economy and invigorated urban markets.

The household contract responsibility system (Xinhua News Agency)

In January 2006, *Regulations on the Agricultural Tax in the PRC* was abolished. Farmers bade farewell to the 2,600-year old *Imperial Rations and State Taxes*. This was another landmark reform after the land reform of the household contract responsibility system in the history of the new China. It played an important role in easing the burden of farmers, increasing their income and incentivizing production. It was also of great significance for speeding up rural economic development, promoting harmony and progress in rural society, liberating rural productive forces, consolidating the elementary position of agriculture, and facilitating coordinated development in urban-rural areas.

China has a large population with relatively little land. The land each household owns is limited. The scale of household land management was the smallest in the world. Household land management could play an important role when rural productive forces were at a low level, but it cannot meet the demands of high-level, large-scale agricultural operations. Such a small scale did not help farmers increase their income; nor was it good for the state to guarantee food security. Managing agriculture on a large scale can achieve twin goals: helping farmers to increase their income; and efficiently augmenting grain supply. This requires that production factors of agriculture, especially land, should be able to be transferred within a proper limit, so as to push forward intensive land management.

In 2013, land usufruct across the nation was registered and confirmed, and corresponding certificates were issued. We improved the registration system for contract and management rights of rural land and strengthened contractual property rights protection and the rights to manage all kinds of rural land, such as arable land and woodland. After certificates of land usufruct were issued, land inventories were activated and the question of what kind of management would maximize the benefits of land usufruct was addressed. Farmers could treat the land as a commodity, freely subleasing, contracting for and mortgaging it. Middlemen, acting in a way similar to supermarkets or commodity dealers, were then needed to put the land certificates in circulation, thereby activating land resources, improving the efficiency of land use and increasing farmers' property income. Under the principle of obeying the law, and on the basis of volunteering and compensating, we guide the rights to contract for and mortgage land so that land can circulate in good order, and develop varied patterns of management on an appropriate scale. We quickly foster new types of participants in agricultural management and offer more support to households that join farm societies, to professional households that run big farms, family farms and farmers' cooperative societies. We are helping farmers to rapidly develop their cooperative societies, and encouraging them to build diversified types of cooperative society such as professional cooperation and joint stock cooperation. We are gradually delivering more agriculture-related projects to cooperative societies. We encourage and support contracted land to flow to households who join their farms, to professional households who run big farms, family farms and farmers' cooperative societies, as mentioned before, in order to innovate the system of agricultural production and management. We will simultaneously establish a rigorous system that allows industrial and commercial enterprises to rent farmers' contracted land and a supervision system to oversee the renting process. We will undertake a nationwide plan to confirm and register the usufruct of rural land and issue corresponding certificates. We will grant farmers more property rights in order to coordinate urban and rural development. We will facilitate equal exchange between urban and rural factors and the fair allocation of public resources.

In 2014, China further adjusted the policy concerning the relocation of registered residence by unifying the urban and rural registration systems and implementing the residence certificate system across the whole country. As social and economic development in urban and rural areas unfolds, it has become a basic requirement to eliminate the differences between urban and rural household registration systems. Fully rescinding the limits on farmers living in designated towns and small cities is now well under way; we will gradually lift the limits on farmers residing in medium-sized cities and create reasonable conditions for people to settle down in big cities while at the same time ensuring that cities do not become too large. In return, we insist on letting industry nurture agriculture and letting cities support rural areas. We adhere to the policy of giving more while taking less and relaxing control. We map out more policies to strengthen, benefit and enrich farmers so that they can participate in the modernization cause and share its fruits. We protect farmers' rights and benefits that are associated with production factors, ensure that rural migrant workers can earn the same pay as others for doing the same work and guarantee that farmers can equally enjoy land value-added income. We are quickening the integration of urban-rural development, focusing on integrating urban-rural planning, infrastructure construction and public services. We are facilitating equal exchange between urban and rural factors and the fair allocation of public resources. We are building a new type of industrial-agricultural and urban-rural relations in which industries support agriculture; cities drive rural areas ahead; industry and agriculture benefit each other and cities and rural areas are integrated.

Second, we reformed the public economy and SOEs. At the early stage of reform, enterprises in places such as Sichuan and Chongqing were given more autonomy as test cases. SOEs were given certain rights to produce, sell, purchase, employ and keep their own profits, which injected vigor and enthusiasm into those enterprises. In 1984, the third plenary session of the 12th central committee of the CPC promoted a systematic strategy for implementing economic system reform and placed a stress on urban economic system reform. The conference proposed to let SOEs be their own masters in production and management after they had been given more rights and profits at an early stage, to implement the 'management contract responsibility system' and the 'manager or factory director responsibility system', and to reform the tax system and enterprise property rights.

In the mid-1990s, the third plenary session of the 14th central committee set the basic direction for the reform of SOEs, which constituted the guideline for economic system reform in the 1990s. Since then, the reform of SOEs, once focused on transferring power and profits, has entered a new phase to transform the system, in the hope of turning them into real market participants. The major measure was pushing forward the establishment of a modern enterprise system in SOEs. It is a necessity for developing socialized mass production and a market economy; and it is the direction for the reform of SOEs. The fundamental feature of a modern enterprise system is the clarification of property rights. The state assets in the enterprises are owned by the state. The enterprises own all corporate property rights including those invested by the state, and are legal entities that enjoy civil rights and bear civil liabilities. With whole corporate property, enterprises run their own businesses in compliance with the law, assume sole responsibility for profits and losses, pay taxes as required, and take responsibility to maintain and increase the value of assets for investors. Corresponding to the value of their investment, investors enjoy ownership rights including the right to earn profits, make big decisions and select managers. If enterprises go bankrupt, investors are liable only for the value of their investment. Enterprises produce and manage themselves according to market demands and take as their sole purpose improving productivity and economic performance. The government does not directly interfere with enterprises' production and management. In market competition, the best enterprises survive. Those that suffer long-term losses and become insolvent should declare bankruptcy in accordance with the law.

We also endeavor to build a scientific enterprise leadership system and a scientific organization and management system, to coordinate relations among investors, operators and employees, and to forge an operation mechanism that combines the functions of incentives and punishments. All enterprises will move in this direction. In addition, we are adjusting the strategic layout of the state-owned economy, reducing the absolutely dominant position held by SOEs in China's economy to a leading position; we are re-classifying SOEs into public, security and competitive categories and are reducing the number of restrictions and relaxing controls over the enterprises that fall into the competitive category. Through reform, SOEs have been integrated into the market economy and must fine-tune themselves to the new trends of marketization and globalization. They have to focus on regulating management decisions, maintaining and increasing the value of their assets, participating in fair competition, improving efficiency and competitive edge, and taking responsibility for society.

Third, we have been actively encouraging the development of the private economy. In 1987, the non-public economy was put forward as a supplement at the 13th National Congress of the CPC. This was the first great leap forward for the non-public economy, which was once called the 'tail of capitalism', to become a supplement to socialism. In 1992, the report of the 14th National Congress of the CPC said that the non-public economy was a beneficial supplement to socialism. In 1997, the 15th National Congress of the CPC proposed that the non-public economy was an important part of the socialist market economy and that efforts were needed to develop it. This was the second great leap forward. Now, the private economy is protected by law and is developing rapidly. While cultivating and developing the private economy, we insist that it should share the same rights and opportunities, and obey the same rules as the state-owned economy. We have abolished many kinds of unreasonable rules and removed many invisible barriers against the private economy. Private enterprises account for 85% of all enterprises and are playing an important role in keeping the economy expanding, promoting innovation, increasing employment and boosting taxes.

Fourth, we have been aggressively developing the mixed ownership economy, in which state-owned, collective and non-public capital cross-hold shares. This is an important part of the basic economic system. It is good for state-owned capital to multiply its function, maintain and increase its value, and enhance its competitiveness. It is good for the various types of capital to draw on each other's advantages and offset their own weaknesses, so as to improve one another and to develop together. More entities in the state-owned economy and other economies with different kinds of ownership are allowed to evolve into mixed ownership. Non-state-owned capital can participate in programs invested with state-owned capital. Employees are permitted to hold shares in their own enterprises in a mixed-ownership economy, forming a community that integrates the interests of capital holders and workers. The economic system no longer has a simple and straightforward structure. An economic structure in which the public-owned economy dominates and a variety of economic elements developing simultaneously has been formed, has put an end to the highly centralized planned economic system and signaled the formation of a management system under which the government regulates only at a macro level while the market is mainly responsible for regulation. Diversified ownership has appeared simultaneously in urban and rural areas. For instance, there is the household contract responsibility system, new business and production participants, and rural households or urban families as market participants. There are rural self-employed households, and specialized households. New types of cooperative economic organization also came into being and developed, such as agricultural cooperatives, stock cooperatives and 'company-cum-farmers' organizations. The number of individual, partnership and family-run companies in cities is huge. Incorporated enterprises are developing rapidly. SOEs have been transformed into public enterprises, becoming leaders of shareholding system reform and real stakeholders in market competition. The property owners of SOEs are diversified. Most SOEs that are now socialized and whose assets are tradable have implemented corporate reform. We encourage non-public enterprises to participate in the reform of SOEs. We encourage developing enterprises with mixed ownership whose controlling stake is held by non-public capital. We encourage competitive private enterprises to partake in modern corporate system construction.

2.2.3 The shaping of an open economic system

The third plenary session of the 11th central committee of the CPC required practicing opening up externally while reforming internally. Over the past 30 years, China has successfully transformed itself from a closed or semi-closed economy into an all-directional, open economy. It has determinedly opened its door to the outside world and become one of the most open countries in the world and an important part of the global market and economy. As early as 1978, Agence France Presse described the third plenary session of the 11th central committee of the CPC as a sign that China had given a green light to the new policy of modernization. The French magazine *Le Point* named Deng Xiaoping as its 1978 figure of the year for opening up China to the world. Through the construction of export-oriented processing zones that were later changed into SEZs, China has adopted a multi-level opening strategy extending from small to larger areas. This was the first crucial point for opening up. In 1979, the Chinese government decided to give special and preferential treatment to Guangdong and Fujian provinces concerning their economic activities with foreign countries; it, too, decided to build SEZs in Shenzhen, Zhuhai, Shantou and Xiamen as windows to attract foreign investment and learn foreign advanced technology and management expertise. These four SEZs are quite close to international markets such as Hong Kong and Macau, have intimate ties with the outside (by being the hometown for many Chinese immigrants), and boast convenient land and sea transportation routes. Meanwhile, they have a vast hinterland economy to bolster their development. In 1984, another 14 coastal cities were allowed to open up: Dalian, Qinhuangdao, Tianjin, Yantai, Qingdao, Lianyungang, Nantong, Shanghai, Ningbo, Wenzhou, Fuzhou, Guangzhou, Zhenjiang and Beihai. These drives to accelerate opening up and draw more foreign investment and advanced technology made them ideal places to set up Sino-foreign joint ventures, cooperative enterprises or wholly foreign-invested enterprises.

In 1988, Hainan province was added to the list of SEZs and became the biggest of its kind in China. In 1990, the Chinese government made a strategic decision to develop and open Pudong new district in Shanghai. This marked another landmark in China's opening-up strategy and since then a new development has emerged. In 1990, Comrade Deng Xiaoping said: "Shanghai is our trump card. Developing Shanghai is a shortcut. Developing Pudong will have a far-reaching impact. It's not just about Pudong but also about the development of Shanghai, and about the development of the Yangtze river delta and the Yangtze river basin by using Shanghai as a base." The development and opening up of Pudong not only shored up the construction of a core area in Shanghai devoted to the international economy, trade, finance and shipping and for Shanghai's rapid economic development, but also heads the economic development of the Yangtze river delta, thereby contributing to the rapid development of the regional economy.

In 2001, the Chinese government, after 13 years of negotiations, finally succeeded in securing the country's accession to the WTO, which was a milestone in reform and opening up. Upon joining the WTO, China committed itself to fully participating in world competition and globalization. This meant fulfilling all the commitments it had made when entering the organization; such a strategy was also highly conducive to increasing the breadth and depth of opening up and to facilitating trade and investment. We pledged to relax the restrictions in foreign trade, to cancel non-tariff measures, such as import quotas and licenses; to continually open the service industries of finance, commerce and telecoms, and to slash tariffs to generally below 10% by 2005. The fact that China became an official member of the WTO in 2001 indicates that it had already become highly integrated into the world economy and that mutual influence was deepening. To be sure, China cannot develop in isolation; nor can the world develop without China. So, we should stick to the basic national policy of opening up. From building SEZs to opening up coastal, riparian, border and inland districts and to joining the WTO, we have been actively coordinating 'bringing in' and 'going out', exploiting domestic and international markets and resources, and comprehensively improving the standard of the open economy. To adapt to the new trend of economic globalization, we must adopt a more proactive open strategy and perfect the open economic system that is mutually beneficial, diversified, balanced, safe and efficient. We should accelerate the establishment of infrastructure links with neighboring countries and regions, push forward the construction of the Silk Road economy, and build a maritime Silk Road, forming a new and multi-dimensional open situation. The purpose is to reform the mode of 'going global', and to grasp the opportunities at a time when global industries are changing. The essence of China (Shanghai) Pilot Free Trade Zone (FTZ) is to create a globalized and legally-based investment climate that is more attractive to high-end industries.

On August 22, 2013, the State Council officially approved the establishment of China (Shanghai) Pilot FTZ. The pilot zone covers an area of 28.78 square kilometers and integrates four existing zones under the special supervision of the Customs – Waigaoqiao FTZ, Waigaoqiao Free Trade Logistics Park, Yangshan Free Trade Port Area and Pudong Airport Comprehensive FTZ. The establishment of Shanghai Pilot FTZ conformed to a new and developing global economic and trade trend and heralded a more proactive open strategy. The zone adopts a market access negative list and allows people to 'do whatever the law does not prohibit'. The zone lays stress on opening the service industry and greatly facilitates trade and investment, promotes the use of the renminbi in cross-border transactions, relaxes controls on foreign currency exchange, and improves the foreign currency exchange management system concerning trade in goods and services. The zone draws on opening up to promote development, reform and innovation, with a view to gaining experience in system innovation that can be replicated and popularized. The essence is to go with the trend of economic globalization and to spur reform and opening up. We unify the laws and rules relating to domestic and foreign capital, retain the stability, transparency and predictability of our policy on foreign capital, and relax restrictions on investment in service industries such as the financial, educational, cultural and medical service sectors. We will gradually permit foreign investment to enter the childcare and elderly care service sectors, in addition to construction and architectural design, accounting and auditing services, logistics and ecommerce. We will further open manufacturing industry and reform the rules by, for example, adopting pre-establishment national treatment and negative list management mode. In abiding by the principle of allowing people 'to do whatever the law does not prohibit', and by adopting the market access negative list and suspending some laws and regulations, the government will be forced to reform and transform itself from a controlling government to one that is disinterested and dedicated to delivering services. Foreign-funded projects outside of negative list are now subject to the filing system instead of the former examination and approval system. We manage foreign investment by records management. To set up a company in the zone, investors only need to register with the industry and commerce department and can decide their capital contributions at their own discretion. The registration system permits them to receive a license before a certificate.

China is actively building a network of FTZs that orients the country to the world. The construction of Guangdong, Tianjin and Fujian FTZs has already taken off. China is negotiating with countries and regions along the 'One Belt, One Road' with regard to building FTZs, to make cooperation more intimate, communication more convenient and interests and stakes more integrated.

2.2.4 Transforming governmental functions at all levels and improving their governing ability

While establishing a socialist market economy, we have also reformed the governmental administrative system. Transforming governmental functions necessitates a profound reform of its institutions. We have been perfecting the government's macro regulation in fields such as the national development strategy, planning and orientation, the balance between total supply and total demand, the coordination among important economic structures, the optimizing of the distribution of productive forces, the mitigating of the influence by economic cycle fluctuation and precaution against systematic risks.

First, we should perfect the administrative operating mechanism in which decision-making power, executive power and supervision power balance and check each other. While executing decision-making power, we must scientifically and seriously practice democratic centralism. If we allow an individual or group of people to make decisions without due consideration, mistakes and even grave consequences will be unavoidable. While exercising executive power, we must be determined and steadfast and act with thunder-like force and wind-like swiftness. If we just talk rather than act, or find excuses to evade our responsibilities, we will waste resources, become lazy and let people down. In order to exercise power strictly, we must be forceful, impartial and incorruptible and act with the force and speed of a thunderbolt. If we pardon law-breakers, or even condone and protect them and assign them important positions, our power will lose legitimacy and credibility and we will fall into crisis.

In 1994, China began to adopt a tax distribution system so as to manage national finance. The essence of a tax distribution system is to match the purse of central and local governments with their power and responsibilities, thus forming a revenue system for central and local governments through tax classification. Based on the principle of combining power, responsibilities and purse, taxes either go to the central or local governments according to their type. The types of tax that are necessary to protect the nation's rights and interests and exercise macro regulation go to the central government; those taxes that directly relate to economic development are generally shared by the central and local governments; those taxes that are suitable for local governments to collect go to the local governments; we are increasing the varieties of local tax to boost the income of local governments. The tax distribution system is a finance management mode widely practiced among market economy countries. It plays a positive role in properly handling distribution relations between the central and local governments, in reinforcing tax collection, protecting financial income and improving the ability to carry out macro regulation.

The new round of fiscal reform aims to pass laws on budgets, publicize budgets, enforce the power of 'checks and balances', and form a modern fiscal system where responsibility and power are in alignment with each other. This is an important guarantee for the modernization of the management system. The reform aims to build a budget management system that is standard, open and transparent; a tax system that is fair, unified and applicable in regulation; and a system where the power and responsibilities of the central and local governments are in proportion to the money they expend. The system should, functionally, adapt to the needs of scientific development and help finance play a better role in stabilizing the economy, delivering public services, adjusting distribution, protecting the environment and safeguarding the nation; it should, in terms of mechanism, meet the new requirements on modernizing the national management system, ensure that power and responsibilities balance and check each other and function efficiently, creating a clear, accountable and sustainable system.

The major components in this area are as follows. First, we should perfect legislation. We should foster the notion of rule of law, manage finance according to the law and bring all financial operations together onto the track of law. Second, we should make power and responsibility transparent. We should reasonably adjust and make clear the power and responsibilities of central and local governments and urge governments at all levels to perform their duties, take responsibility and do their utmost.

Second, we should transform the government into one that provides services, enforces the law and is accountable for what it does. We should optimize governmental rules and regulations, limit its duties and improve its operational procedures. We should push the government to transform itself from being a body capable of 'doing everything' to a public service-oriented entity. We should build a macro regulatory system that generally employs indirect tools to realize its policies. At first, we should ensure that all economies with different types of ownership have equal access to production factors and are equally protected by the law. We should uphold the equality of rights, opportunities and rules, abolish all types of unreasonable rules against non-public economies and remove all kinds of invisible barriers. Then, we should make market rules that are fair, open and transparent: we should unify the market admittance system, so that all market participants can equally enter the fields outside of the negative list in line with the law; we should unify market supervision, and abolish all practices hindering fair competition. The government should make business registration more convenient, change the verification system into a registration system, permit investors to get a license before receiving a certificate, not vice versa, and gradually allow investors to decide their own registered capital instead of compelling them to submit a certain amount of registered capital. We should deepen investment reform, and give enterprises real investment autonomy: enterprises can decide their own investment programs following the laws and rules and will be subject to less adjustment and fewer examining procedures; no examination and approval is needed except for programs concerning national and ecological security, the national mapping of important productive forces, the exploitation of strategic resources and significant public interest. Finally, we should do a better job in devising and implementing development strategies, plans, policies and standards, in supervising market activities and in offering all kinds of public service. We should enhance central government accountability and its ability to execute macro regulation and increase the local governments' sense of responsibility in providing public services, market supervision, social management and environmental protection. We should implement the reform of income distribution and tax, create a fair market environment for competition among all types of enterprises, and focus on stimulating the various market participants to bring about new vitality. We should simplify administrative procedures, delegate powers to lower levels, deepen reform of the administrative approval system, decrease central government management over small businesses as much as possible, and cancel all approval procedures relating to economic areas where the market mechanism functions perfectly. As for the remaining administrative approval procedures, we should standardize them and improve their efficiency. As for the many and extensive local and social issues that directly relate to the grassroots, we should leave them all to local and basic-level governments. We should encourage governments to purchase services. In principle, as far as everyday living services are concerned, the government will introduce competition and purchase them from society by way of contract or commission. As for those items that still need approval, the government will publicize a list of them, defining clearly the bans and constraints. Freedom is given to those items outside the list so long as the law does not prohibit them. The government has to be able to resist interference. The visible hands should be 'seen less'. The hand of government should not compete with the hand of the market for power, or try to replace it. We should respect the invisible hand and let it expand. The government should extend more powers to enterprises and adopt the 'three-aspect' policy: first, it should relax control and reduce examination and approval which means power, control and interests; second, it should open up, allow private capital to enter the financial market, and break 'ceilings' or 'glass doors'; third, it should open the market and give full play to the role of the market. We should make the government function well in protecting property rights, building a sound legal system and guaranteeing a decent livelihood for the people.

Third, the transformation from 'governmental control' to 'governmental management' represents great progress in state governance theory and methods. To fully grasp the effectiveness of governmental management, we need to take special note of three aspects: first, government structure should be scientific and rational; second, the functions of government should be scientific and reasonable; third, the patterns and methods of governmental management should be scientific and reasonable. State management ability means the ability to use the state system to manage all matters of society, including social stability and development, domestic and foreign affairs, national defense, and the management of the party, the state and the army. The transformation from control to management stresses the pluralism of the managing entities and includes a variety of entities such as the government, enterprises, the market and social organizations to manage using various methods. The transformation also emphasizes democratic management. To put in place administrative and social management, we not only need governmental authority but also have to rely on non-governmental organizations (NGOs), the internet, cooperation and negotiation to manage public affairs. The transformation requires us to build a modernized social legal system and the rule of law; to handle social affairs according to the law, to normalize procedures and contracts, and to develop innovative ways to manage.

Chapter 3

What are the Major Achievements of China's Economic Reform?

The approach that China has adopted in practicing a market economy contains some unique characteristics. They include its time-honored history, its large population, its vast territory and the leadership of the CPC. As a new member of the global market economy, and while learning from the models and modes of other market economies, China has made innovations in building its socialist market economy. In doing so, it has created an alternative example, different to the one being practiced in the west, for other countries with their own cultures and histories to emulate.

3.1 Continuous, steady and rapid economic growth

First, China's economy continues to grow at a high speed. In 2009, the *US News and World Report* commented that the world had become accustomed to China's rapid economic growth and that its miracle had turned into a norm. China's economy has been developing fast since the start of the reform and opening-up policy. From 1978 to 2012, its GDP increased by 9.8% a year on average, making China the fastest-growing economy in the world. In the 35 years since the beginning of reform and opening up, the total value of China's economy has risen 142-fold, ranking second in the world, and enabling it to secure a position among middle-income countries. China has become more involved in the global economy. Its foreign trade has grown 186-fold, with the value of its exports topping the world in 2012. China's foreign exchange reserves ranked first for seven consecutive years. It has influenced the world economy greatly. From 2008 to 2012, it contributed more than 20% annually on average to the growth of the world economy, becoming an important force in facilitating the global economic recovery.

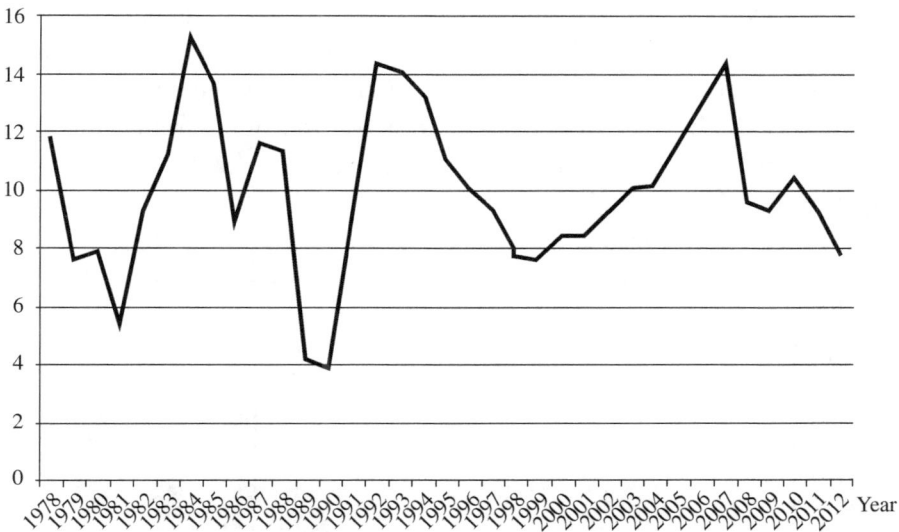

Figure 1-1 GDP Growth Rates from 1978 to 2012 (%)

(Source: *GDP Growth Rates from 1978 to 2012*, National Bureau of Statistics)

China's economic development was like an engine to world economic growth following the 2008 financial crisis. The IMF's *World Economic Outlook* issued on October 1, 2009 said that Asian countries including China were leading the economic recovery. Although China's GDP has risen to the second largest in the world, it remains a developing country, with 40m people still living below the official poverty line and earning the equivalent of less than one dollar a day. As early as the 1980s, the American economist Paul Samuelson said that China was an economic giant deep in slumber, and that it would overtake Japan and become second only to the US before 2005 if it found an effective mode of growth. At the same time, Alexander Lukin, head of the Center for East Asian Studies at Moscow State Institute of International Relations, thought that Deng Xiaoping not only managed to lead China onto the right road but also enlightened socialism across the whole world.

Second, economic structural adjustment and industrialization are moving ahead rapidly. Since reform and opening up, as a late-industrialized country, China has made good use of its factor endowments related to industrialization and set an example to the world of fast industrialization. China has grown out of the middle period of industrialization and entered into the late period. This marks a milestone in China's process of industrialization. In 2010, a comprehensive index of industrialization in east China reached 80, indicative of the middle-late period of industrialization; the same index for northeast China was 50, putting it in the middle period; while the same index for central and west China was 35 and 30, respectively, also placing these regions in the middle period. The levels of industrialization were declining from the east, to the northeast, the center and west. Development was clearly geographically imbalanced in China.

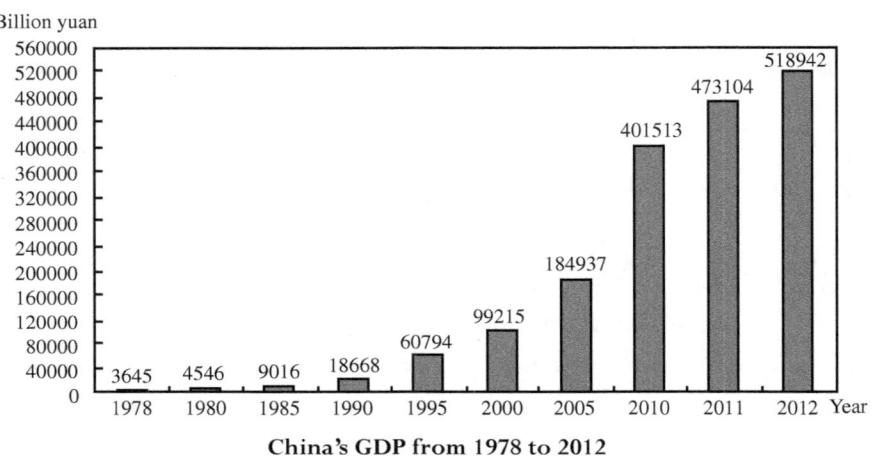

China's GDP from 1978 to 2012

'Chinese manufacturing' has become recognized and accepted across the world. China has become a large, emerging industrial country; over the last 35 years, its industrialization has never stopped forging ahead. It has become a major manufacturing country from a backward agricultural one. World Bank data reveals that China accounted for 17.6% of the world's added value of manufacturing industry in 2010. According to the international standard industrial classification, China is the largest producer in the world of seven out of 22 different industries. Its output of more than 220 kinds of industrial products is ranked first. Besides the output of traditional industrial products such as steel, coal, cement and chemical fertilizer, the output of grain, meat, un-ginned cotton, peanuts, tea and fruit are also in first place. Rapeseed, sugarcane and soybean production ranks second, third and fourth, respectively. A group of large, internationally competitive enterprises has quickly emerged and many enterprises now rank among the Fortune 500. In 2000, no Chinese company appeared in the world's top 10 mechanical engineering companies, and only three among the top fifty. In 2011, there were three Chinese companies in the top 10, and 11 in the top 50. Between 2005 and 2011, there was a clear trend for European and American companies to slide down the list of the world's top 50 mechanical engineering companies, except for a few established, strong companies such as Caterpillar, Volvo and Liebherr. Meanwhile, Chinese companies were ascending with great force and speed.

China is the largest producer and seller of new electronic products, such as computers, mobile phones and modern durable consumer goods such as color televisions, fridges and cars. The dramatic increase in Chinese exports has allowed global consumers to purchase a variety of goods at the 'Chinese price'. However, most international consumers are unable to recall a single Chinese brand name, a sign that that China is only a large manufacturing country, as opposed to a powerful one, and that it remains short of world-famous enterprises and products.

We have retooled our industrial structure. Over the last 35 years of reform and opening up, all the three broad economic sectors have achieved great growth. The fundamental position of agriculture has been under constant reinforcement; industry has kept on developing rapidly; the service sector is expanding swiftly. From 1979 to 2012, the value added of the primary, secondary and tertiary economic sectors has increased by 4.6%, 11.3% and 10.8%, respectively. The ratio of value added of the three economic sectors changed from 28.2:47.9:23.9 in 1978 to 10.1:45.3:44.6 in 2012. The percentage of the tertiary economic sector went up to 46.1% in 2013, surpassing the secondary sector for the first time, reflecting the fact that the industrial structure is constantly improving.

The growth rate and proportion of secondary and tertiary industries from 2002 to 2012

Year	Growth rate		Proportion of GDP	
	Secondary economic sector	Tertiary economic sector	Secondary economic sector	Tertiary economic sector
2002	9.90%	7.30%	51.70%	33.70%
2003	12.50%	6.70%	52.90%	32.30%
2004	11.10%	8.30%	53.00%	31.80%
2005	11.40%	9.60%	47.30%	40.30%
2006	12.50%	10.30%	48.70%	39.50%
2007	13.40%	11.40%	49.20%	39.10%
2008	9.30%	9.50%	48.60%	40.10%
2009	9.50%	8.90%	46.80%	42.60%
2010	12.20%	9.50%	46.80%	43.00%
2011	10.60%	8.90%	46.80%	43.10%
2012	8.10%	8.10%	45.30%	44.60%

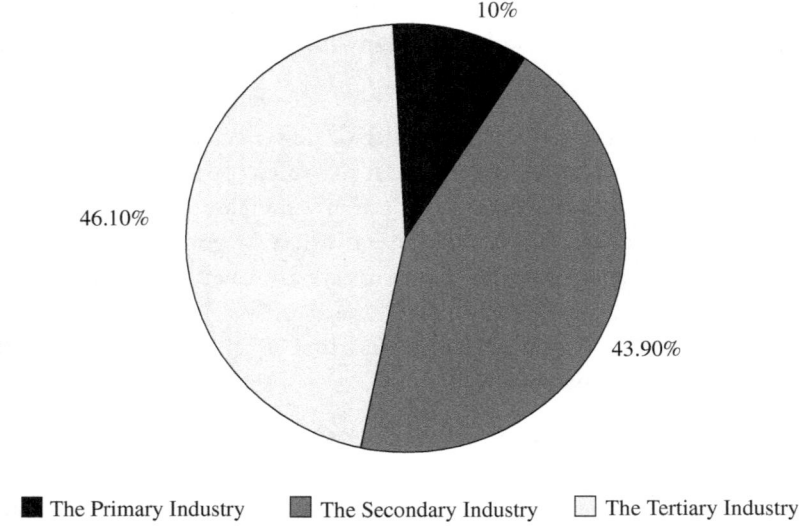

■ The Primary Industry ■ The Secondary Industry □ The Tertiary Industry

The proportion of primary, secondary and tertiary industries in 2013

Source: *A Structural Comparison of the Three Economic Sectors in 2002, 2012 and 2013* (National Bureau of Statistics)

Since the beginning of the 21st century, China's new and high-tech industry and modern service industry have been performing unusually well. In 2011, the total output of 'large' new and high-tech manufacturing companies was valued at Rmb9,200bn, second highest in the world. The output of major new and high-tech products such as mobile phones, color televisions, computers and some medicines ranked first. China has launched 70 high-tech projects in areas such as integrated circuit design and satellite navigation, which has attracted more than Rmb440bn of social investment. Many new industries that are well equipped and with obvious advantages are emerging, becoming new growth points of industrial development. In 2011, China's exports of new and high-tech products were worth US$548.8bn, accounting for 39% of all its exports, and ranking first in the world. To sum up, China has become a huge industrial country, but not yet a powerful one in terms of industrial structure. To become a strong, rather than just a large industrial country, China needs to make good, strategic choices in fields such as research, development and design, technological support, human resources and protection of property rights.

Third, infrastructure has developed rapidly. Transportation facilities are improving day by day. Expressways, railways, airports and urban public utilities have changed enormously. Over the past 35 years, China's traffic network has constantly expanded, transportation capacity strengthened and transportation efficiency improved, providing strong support for the development of all industries. In 2012, China's length of railways in operation reached 98,000km, 88.8% longer than in 1978 and the second longest in the world; the length of highways reached 4,240,000km, 3.8 times longer than in 1978; the length of civil aviation routes was 3,280,000km, 21 times longer; the length of oil and gas pipelines was 90,000km, 9.9 times longer; cargo throughput of major ports was 6.65bn tons, 32.5 times greater, and the largest total in the world for several years in succession. Some modernized communication and transportation facilities emerged from scratch and grew rapidly. At the beginning of reform and opening up, there were no expressways in China; in 2012, the length of China's expressways had reached 96,200km, the second highest total in the world. High-speed rail has developed rapidly, and trains appeared with a top speed of 350 kph, demonstrating the advanced nature of China's railways. In 2012, the high-speed railway network measured 9,356km, the longest in the world. The Korean newspaper *JoonAng Daily* commented on its website: "China's development is as rapid as a high-speed train and this will soon become the speed of global development."[1]

Its informatization project has enabled China to construct a basic national network of information and communication, which, complete with advanced technology, covers the whole nation, accesses the world and offers comprehensive services. The scale of the post and telecoms business is expanding, as is the range of service sectors. The scale of the internet, speed of growth and the number of network users rank first in the world.

The continuing perfection of the urban-rural commodity circulation network has improved the rural modern commodity circulation network. The rural consumption environment has improved through the introduction of urban circulation enterprises, rural chain stores and logistics distribution centers in rural areas and by the perfection of the circulation network that enables industrial products to enter rural areas easily. By the end of 2012, according to the National Bureau of Statistics, 600,000 countryside stores had been built or transformed across the nation, covering 75% of all administrative villages.

Fourth, urbanization has been forging ahead rapidly. Over the last 30 years since the beginning of reform and opening up, China's level of urbanization has risen quickly. Up to the end of 2011, the urbanization rate of Beijing,

---

[1] *Cited from Chinese Motivation Net, www.zhlzw.com*

Tianjin, Shanghai and Guangdong had each exceeded 68%, and the rate in remote provinces such as Xinjiang, Yunnan and Gansu had exceeded 33%. From a spatial perspective, the urbanization of China's three major regions has differed, with each having its own specific advantages. Although China's urbanization is continuously moving forward and the general level of urbanization is close to 51%, the rate remains quite unbalanced among different regions; there is a gap of 70% between the highest and lowest levels. Geographically, it can be divided into three broad regions: the highly urbanized eastern coastal region, the moderately urbanized inland middle region, and the lowly urbanized inland western region. *A Blue Book About Society in 2012* released by the sociology department of The Chinese Academy of Social Sciences pointed out that the percentage of China's urban population had exceeded that of its rural population in 2011 for the first time ever over the past thousands of years. That year was a milestone in the history of China's urbanization, indicating that our nation had already entered a new growth period that is centered on urban society.

3.2 Rapidly improving living standards

First, as incomes rise fast, society has made a historical leap forward from a dearth of food and clothing to a general wellbeing, and is now moving towards a quality life on all fronts. Through deepening the reform of income distribution by bringing about an increase in incomes in step with the development of the economy, an increase in wages in accordance with an improvement in productivity and maintaining a balance between efficiency and equality, we have ensured that the income and wealth of both urban and rural people have increased rapidly. In 2012, urban per capita disposable income was Rmb24,565, 71 times more than in 1978 and an average increase of 13.4% year-on-year, or an inflation-adjusted rise of 7.4%. The rural net income per capita was Rmb7,919, 58 times more than in 1978, an annual growth of 12.8%, or an inflation-adjusted rise of 7.5%. The wealth owned by urban and rural people increased significantly. China's GDP per capita reached US$6,000 in 2012, and is now nearing US$10,000, showing that China has grown from a poor country with low average mean incomes into a developing country with a low-medium income. The report of the 18th National Congress of the CPC proposed to build an all-round well-off society in 2020 and a modern socialist country that is rich, strong, democratic, civilized and harmonious in 2050 so as to realize the grand rejuvenation of the Chinese nation. From 'fixing a shortage of food and clothing' to 'reasonable prosperity'; from 'general well-being' to an 'all-round quality life';

Chapter 3

and from 'constructing comprehensively' to 'comprehensively accomplishing construction', we can see that it is both a motivation mandate and a guideline for action. The most eye-catching statement was to double GDP and incomes. In 2010, urban per capita disposable income was Rmb19,109 and rural per capita net income was Rmb5,919. This reflected our priority to put people first coupled with their desire to get rich. We should not only double GDP, but also double incomes. The target of doubling income is feasible, not unachievable.

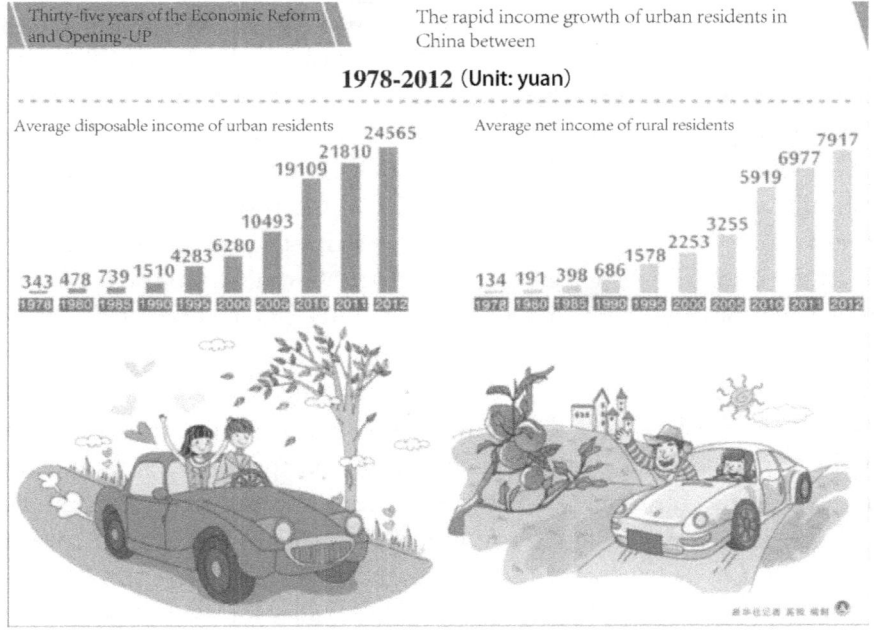

Urban and rural incomes have increased fast in the 35 years of reform and opening up

Second, life has become more colorful and the quality of life has improved. China is gradually becoming a major sales terminal of the global consumer market. Improvements in social security and urbanization will bring about huge effective demands. At present, commodities in the market are numerous in type, large in number and clearly improved in quality. All kinds of commodities are available for eating, wearing and using, satisfying people's varied demands at all levels. Over the past 30 years, great achievements have been made in demand-oriented production and operation. Effective supplies are continuously rising. A buyer's market has formed and today's consumers have more freedom and choices in shopping. In particular, IT products such as mobile phones and computers, cars, home furniture and household appliances that help improve living conditions and quality of life have increased greatly. They make commodity demand-supply structure more reasonable and people's choices more diversified.

The Engel coefficient of urban residents has fallen with each passing year, from 57.5% in 1978 to 36.3% in 2007. The government has abolished the agricultural tax, built a social security system that is closely related to people's livelihoods and covers education, medical care, housing and so on, and successfully made the leap from sufficiency in food and clothing to quality of life. Commodities in the market are in very ample supply. Consumer demand is varied and keeps on increasing. In the 1980s, people used to buy bicycles, watches and sewing machines. In the 1990s, they liked to buy fridges, washing machines and televisions. Today, they buy cars, houses and high-end durable goods. The change from the 'old three domestic appliance items' to the 'new three items' reflects that, with the improvement in living standards and the satisfaction of people's need for eating, clothing and using, the consumer focus has shifted to travel, lifestyle and health; the consumption structure is constantly being upgraded. Among the major commodities, sales of cars, telecoms equipment, construction and decorating materials, household electric appliances, audio devices and jewelry have enjoyed the highest annual growth. As the income of urban and rural citizens has risen greatly and consumption capacity has strengthened, the scale of the consumer goods market is continuously expanding and has maintained a tendency to rise steadily and quickly. In 2012, the average living area for each urban resident was 32.9 square meters, 26.2 square meters more than in 1978; the average living area for each rural resident was 37.1 square meters, 29 square meters more than in 1978. The quality of houses has improved and so have the living environment and supporting facilities.[2] The areas of consumption are expanding. Material life is getting more colorful. Durable consumer goods such as color TVs, fridges, air conditioners and mobile phones are gradually making their way into nearly every household. Many more people now own high-end durable consumer goods such as cars and computers.

The impoverished population in urban and rural areas has shrunk greatly. In 2005, the government implemented rural tax reform, canceling the 'three deductions and five plans' policy and reducing or removing agricultural tax. Therefore, farmers say: "No tax for farming, no fee for schooling, but

---

[2] *Cited from Chinese Motivation Net, www.zhlzw.com*

medical reimbursement for us, and only farmers benefit." Since 2006, the government has been directly subsidizing farmers for producing grain, and making cooperative medical services cover almost all rural areas, in addition to offering rural children free compulsory education. With reform and opening up, the impoverished rural population has decreased from 250m in 1978 to 40m in 2010. According to UN statistics, 92% of the world population that had shaken off poverty up to the end of 2005 were Chinese.

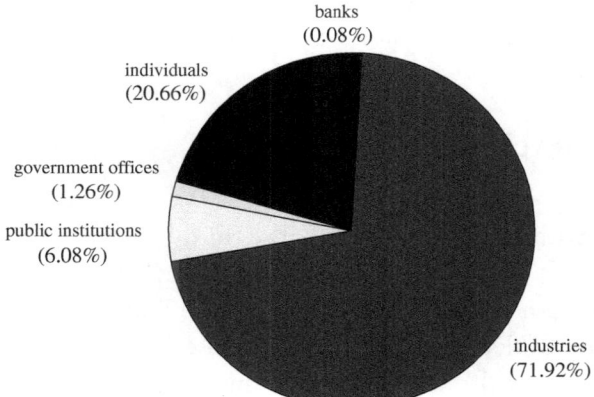

A comparison of the number of people joining the urban basic old-age insurance program categorized according to their occupations in 2011

Third, we have systemized education, health care and social security that used to exist at low levels and we are now endeavoring to make these systems cover the whole nation. We have already made compulsory nine-year education universal across the nation and are now focusing on balancing the development of compulsory education. In 2012, fiscal expenditure for education reached Rmb2,200bn, about Rmb600bn more than the year before. The objective that educational expenditure should account for 4% of China's GDP will be realized on schedule. The urban and rural medical security system covers more than 1.3bn people. Since 2011, the central government has spent Rmb76bn on maintaining the stable operation of the new rural cooperative medical system and the urban basic medical insurance system. The average financial allowance for each person has risen from Rmb120 to Rmb200. All these measures have helped improve the urban and rural medical assistance system. The central government has also spent money on enhancing the ability to provide public health services across the nation and in equalizing public health services. China's basic old-age insurance program covers urban employees in all types of enterprise. All urban enterprises and employees have an obligation to pay the basic old-age insurance premiums. At present, enterprises should pay around 20% of total salaries, while employees should pay 8% of their salaries. A part of the basic old-age insurance premiums paid by enterprises is used to set up mutual funds while the rest goes to personal accounts; and the insurance premiums paid by individuals go entirely to their personal accounts. Up to the end of 2011, 284m people had joined the basic old-age insurance program for urban employees. We have started a new rural cooperative medical system that covers 98.3% of the rural population. Some 21,435,000 urban residents and 53,445,000 rural residents have received the government's minimum living guarantee.[3]

3.3 Rapid development of the mixed ownership economy

The report of the 14th National Congress of the CPC in 1992 mentioned "the economy with mixed ownership". The third plenary session of the 14th central committee of the CPC in 1993 required that SOEs should reform and build a modern cooperate system with "clearly defined property rights". Soon afterwards, SOEs underwent a new large-scale wave of reform. The goal of the reform centered on establishing a modern cooperative system. The third plenary session of the 16th central committee of the CPC proposed to strive to develop the economy with mixed ownership. The third plenary session of the 18th central committee of the CPC clearly allowed non-public enterprises to take part in the reform of SOEs, encouraged developing mixed-ownership enterprises partly invested by non-public capital and allowed mixed-ownership enterprises to give shares to their employees so as to form a community in which capital owners and employees shared the same interests; this created good conditions for private investors to hold shares. In fact, China is now an economy with mixed ownership. Different types of economic ownership coexisting in society marks the economic and social structure of an economy with mixed ownership. Since the beginning of reform and opening up, incessant institutional supply has provided 'space of policy' for capital to become socialized. The 15th National Congress of the CPC, which proposed the idea of an economy with mixed ownership, the 17th National Congress of the CPC, which stressed the development of a mixed ownership economy 'based on the modern property rights system' and the third plenary session of the 18th central committee of the CPC, which re-emphasized that a largely 'state-owned economy and economy with other types of ownership are allowed to develop into one with mixed ownership'

---

[3] Cited from Chinese Motivation Net, www.zhlzw.com

opened up the space of policy and provided a lasting and systematic guarantee for the development of an economy with mixed ownership. In addition, with the gradual removal of systematic barriers and with the market environment getting friendlier by the day, the socialization of capital has gathered 'external momentum'.

Mixed ownership takes on a variety of forms such as the shareholding and shareholding cooperative systems. There are also many ways to realize public ownership. State-owned capital is mostly invested in significant industries and key sectors associated with national security and the lifeline of the national economy; it is also utilized to constantly enhance the vitality, dominance and impact of the state-owned economy. China encourages, endorses and guides the laws and policies concerning the development of the non-public economy to become more sound and sophisticated so that it can ensure that an economy featuring all kinds of ownership can equally use production factors, participate in fair market competition and enjoy protection under the law. For example, there is the rural household contract system, new types of business entity, the rural household or household farming system, new cooperative economic organizations such as cooperatives and stock cooperatives, and an urban private economy that includes the individual economy, partnership businesses, family businesses, and incorporated enterprises that develop and innovate rapidly. SOEs have deepened the reform, got incorporated, diversified their ownership and become real market participants.

Enterprises with mixed ownership are effective micro carriers of the system beneficial to capital socialization. We have pushed forward the reform of the property rights system in SOEs through spreading the mixed ownership mode. There are three aspects of the reform: first, to continue to carry forward corporate system reform in SOEs, especially in large and medium-sized enterprises, so as to diversify the investors and types of ownership of SOEs; second, to give play to the leading role and leverage effect of state-owned capital; third, to let state-owned and non-state-owned enterprises compete fairly and to treat them equally in terms of property rights, market access, government supervision and so on. From the perspective of a socialist market economy, the SOE by nature is an economic rather than a political organization. Shareholding system reform of SOEs can bring about an organic combination of state ownership with market economy and can help SOEs find a mode that effectively boosts productivity. How do you build a social coexistence system? How do you balance the power and interests between the state and private shareholders? How do you realize and balance the controlling power and discourse power of the state and private shareholders and their agents?

The question of how to materialize the interests of the state and private shareholders and their agents is both a theoretical and practical problem. While reforming, we actively encourage non-public enterprises to take part in the reform of SOEs and encourage the development of mixed-ownership enterprises controlled by non-public capital. A mixed-ownership economy in which state-owned capital, collective capital and non-public capital hold shares in each other and mix with each other is a significant form of the basic economic system. It is good for state-owned capital to magnify its functions, maintain and increase its value and raise its competitiveness, and it is good for all capital of different types of ownership to draw on each other's strengths to make up for their own shortcomings, to improve each other and to develop together. We allow an economy dominated by state ownership and other types of ownership to develop into one with mixed ownership. We support employees of mixed-ownership enterprises to hold shares in their enterprises to form a community that integrates the interests of capital holders and workers.

3.4 The shaping of a unified and open market with orderly competition

Economies with different types of ownership develop together. A pluralist market competition pattern has effectively formed. The market has become the basic means of resource distribution. The decisive role of the market in allocating resources is becoming more and more evident.

First, the market system is complete. We have built a consumer goods market at different levels. A market of production factors such as labor, land, capital and technology has developed. Factor markets such as the labor market, capital market, technology market and futures market have developed rapidly. The market transaction system and market culture have formed and have been further perfected. For example, the capital market is not only a significant financing platform, but is also gradually becoming an important platform that creates wealth for the whole of society. The marketization of interest rates and exchange rates is going on. We have canceled the floor on the loan rate and the ceiling on deposit rates. A deposit insurance system is under construction. The marketization of the benchmark deposit rate is being pushed forward. We allow capable private capital to set up financial institutions such as medium-sized or small banks. The marketization entry-exit mechanism for financial institutions is being perfected. A multi-level capital market system is forming. A verification system of stock public offerings has been reformed. We are now implementing a reform to make the renminbi capital account convertible. At the end of 2013, there were 2,356 listed companies in China, and the market capitalization total was Rmb23,560bn, in the world's top three; the annual transaction volume of the futures market exceeded Rmb560,000bn. Land usufruct can be leased; the commodity characteristics of urban land are becoming more obvious. Transactions of land usufruct are becoming more common. The emerging land market has become an important part of the market economy. The labor market is becoming the strongest pillar of economic development. Reform and opening up has: broken the management system in which graduates were appointed to certain positions by the government and then owned by their workplaces or departments; perfected the two-way selection mechanism in which employers and graduates can choose each other at their own discretion; allowed the mechanism of demand-supply, price and competition to play a role in the distribution of human resources; formed a vigorous employment mechanism in which employees can get promoted or demoted and can come and go so that qualified employees get promoted and the unqualified get demoted. Thus, the concept of the 'iron rice bowl' is broken and civil servants and public institution personnel are motivated to be more creative. Under the guidance of labor system reform and the market, we have solved the systematic shortcomings that shackle people's creativity, made a series of systems that can motivate people, liberated people's creativity, let the market play a basic role in distributing talent and facilitated a reasonable circulation of talent. We have let the market play a guiding role in determining the price of the factors of technological research and in distributing innovative factors. The technology market is developing and the mechanism of technology transfer is becoming more sound. Financing conditions for small and medium-sized technological enterprises are improving, as is the mechanism of venture investment. Business models are innovating. With different types of market connecting and interacting with each other, a modern market system is forming that is systematically complete, mechanically sound, unified and open, and with orderly competition, so that transactions of all kinds of commodity can be carried out in the most efficient way.

Second, different kinds of business have advanced alongside each other and new forms of business compete with each other for development. During these years, different types of business such as exclusive stores, specialty stores, supermarkets, convenience stores, department stores and outlets have mushroomed, showing vitality and maintaining steady development. Exclusive stores and specialty stores have strong growth momentum. Shopping malls have become an important feature of the retail market. E-companies have rapidly emerged. Chain operation and ecommerce as means of modern circulation have become the main methods of operation and organization adopted by commercial enterprises. E-business and chain business are gradually developing and growing stronger, with their number multiplying and their size increasing. China has developed all aspects of foreign trade and formed trading relations with most countries and districts in the world. It has set up a total of 163 bilateral economic and trade cooperation rules and regulations, signed 129 bilateral investment agreements and 10 free-trade agreements. Trade partners have increased from just dozens of countries and districts to 231 countries and districts at present. The EU, the US, Asean, Japan and BRIC countries have become China's major trade partners. China has become an important part of the global market. It is now the world's largest exporter, second largest importer, second largest destination of foreign direct investment and fifth largest capital exporting country. The status of China in global and regional economic cooperation is becoming more and more crucial. China has facilitated the establishment and development of the cooperative mechanism for Apec, China, Japan and South Korea, Asean 10+3 and the five central Asian countries and, through international institutions and platforms such as the G20 and WTO, has actively taken part in global economic management, has confronted global challenges together with the international community and has shared development opportunities.

Third, fair, open and transparent market rules are being formed. The crucial problem with economic system reform is handling the relationship between the government and the market. This requires the respect of market law, the further development and perfection of the market transaction system and market culture, and allowing the government to play a better role based on the spirit of contract, freedom of transaction and fairness of competition. The government has passed laws to guarantee equal legal protection and equal access to production factors for all types of economic ownership; it has been adhering to the equality of rights, opportunities and rules, abolished all kinds of unreasonable rules against the non-public economy and removed all types of invisible barriers. The government has unified the system of market admittance so that all market participants can equally enter fields outside of the negative list according to the law. The government has unified market supervisory methods and removed all practices that impair fair competition. The government has rendered business registration more convenient, changed the verification system into a registration system, permitted investors to receive a license before a certificate, but not vice versa, and gradually enabled the registration system to allow investors to decide on registered capital instead of compelling them to submit a certain amount of registered capital. The government has unified the laws and rules relating to domestic and foreign capital, maintained stability of its foreign capital policy, and implemented transparent, predictable and relaxed restrictions on investment in service industries such as financial, educational, cultural and medical services. The government has adopted a pre-establishment national treatment and negative list management mode. It has put into practice the principle of allowing people 'to do whatever the law does not prohibit', has adopted the negative list management mode and has suspended some laws and regulations. A market economy is one regulated by laws, as is required by its nature. Only the market economy can provide the economic base for a modern legal system to emerge and evolve. The more advanced a market economy, the more developed its legal system will be. A market economy needs to admit and respect the autonomy of market participants and to ensure their equal status. A market economy is a contract-based economy. The contract is the prototype of law in the market. The most common legal characteristic of a market economy is the contractual economic relationship. It is through competition that a market economy winnows out weak and backward enterprises and rationally distributes resources. However, competition must be fair and legal; otherwise, the market mechanism will become disorderly or distorted.

Fourth, China's economy has entered into a new normal phase. After more than 30 years of rapid growth, the economy is facing adjustment and transformation. The comparative advantage of cheap labor and land is fading away; the population is ageing; the rural laborforce surplus is diminishing; the economies of scale that have reduced production costs are losing momentum; economic growth will rely more on the quality of human capital and technological advancements; consumption now takes on new features: personalized and diversified consumption has become the mainstream. All these factors have led to a slowing down in growth speed from high to medium-high. The economic structure is constantly upgrading and becoming optimized, with the service sector and consumer demand gradually taking on the major role. In 2014, consumption expenditure contributed 48.5% to China's economic growth, surpassing investment. The value-added of the service sector accounted for 46.7%, outperforming the secondary sector once again. The role of new industries, the service sector and small and micro enterprises are becoming all the more important. Miniaturization, intelligence and professionalization now characterize the organization of industry. High and new technology industries and the manufacturing equipment industry are growing significantly quicker than the national industrial average. The driving forces of the economy are diversified. Factors and investment are being replaced by innovation as the major driving force. China is coordinating and pushing forward new industrialization, urbanization, informatization and agricultural modernization, which has increased the importance of internal consumer demand and has facilitated a reduction in the country's dependence on exports. This is welcome since an excessive dependence on exports may generate external risks. The investment in infrastructure has been upgraded. Opportunities for investing in new technologies, new products, and new business modes and models are emerging in abundance. While high quality foreign investment is being introduced, China is also making investments in foreign countries.

Fifth, the government is transforming itself from a dominating government to a law-abiding and service-oriented one. The major tasks for macro regulation are to balance economic supply and demand, facilitate economic structural coordination, optimize the planning of economic productivity, reduce the impact of economic cyclical fluctuation, take precautions against regional and systematic risks, stabilize market expectations and maintain a sustained and healthy economic growth. Macro regulation takes the state development strategies and planning as the guideline and fiscal and monetary policies as the major tools. The government has built mechanisms for making macro regulation objectives and for using policy tools. The government has reinforced coordination between fiscal and monetary policies and the policies associated with industry and price. The government has tried to perfect the macro-regulatory system. The government adopts economic, legal and other administrative means but, when regulating the macro economy, it relies more on economic means such as monetary, fiscal and industrial policies based on market parameters including price, interest rate, tax level, exchange rate, salary and total tax revenue. The government marketizes the tools of macro regulation, such as the marketization of interest rates and exchange rates. The marketization of resource price is being perfected. The policy tools regulating market economic operation are becoming diversified. The interest rate, reserve requirement ratio, exchange rate and discount rate have frequently been put into use. The operating rules in international markets have also come into play. China obtains external resources from the international market, such as capital, resources, knowledge, systems, technology and even entrepreneurship, which is becoming more common. And Chinese enterprises are moving towards the global market. The government uses fiscal and industrial policies to adjust the supply-demand structure. The industrial structure is being adjusted, and tax policies are drawn on to adjust distribution and industrial development.

Chapter 4

What are the Basic Practices of Deepening Reform and Opening Up in China?

China is a 'vast, transforming and developing country'. Put another way, three characteristics define China: vast, transforming and developing. It is because of the high complexity and difficulty in finding solutions to its development problems that China has taken the reasonable step of choosing a reform path that is gradual yet progressive. And it is by persistently and comprehensively deepening reform and opening up that China has been able to create the miracle of 35 years of rapid growth and an enormous improvement in people's quality of life. The most fundamental lesson that China has learned from more than three decades of experience is bringing about the internal unification of reform, development and stability. We maintain that reform is the momentum of development and the foundation of long-term stability; that development is the purpose of reform and the most reliable guarantee of stability; and that stability is a precondition for reform and development as well as an important requirement of development. In short, the momentum of reform is unstoppable; as the purpose, development cannot slow down; as the precondition, stability cannot weaken.

4.1 Reform and opening up is a source of vigor for contemporary China to develop and progress

China's reform and opening up has provided robust momentum and shored up modernization, serving as a source of vigor for contemporary China to develop and progress. It has been proven that reform and opening up was a crucial choice determining the fate of contemporary China and a major factor helping China to make big strides in keeping pace with the times. Reform means breaking all thoughts, concepts and systems that shackle the development of productivity and seeking roads and methods that are favorable for development. Opening up in parallel with reform means opening up the gateway, communicating with other countries and flowing into the stream of world civilization. Therefore, opening up is also a type of reform, not only providing experience and wisdom for reform, but also propelling it forward. There are many reasons for China's success in reforming. In terms of ideas and focuses, China is not unique.

4.1.1 The idea of persistently deepening reform and opening up

Reform won't stop, and nor will opening up. While pushing forward reform and opening up, China adheres to the following four significant ideas.

First, it adheres to the idea of reforming gradually and 'crossing the river by fumbling for stones as footholds'. Fumbling for stones when we cross the river means fumbling for laws and regulations. We try out new reforming measures and then make summaries before popularizing them nationwide. This kind of methodology is not only good for activating innovative enthusiasm and creativity at the grassroots level, for finding the right solutions to problems and controlling reforming risks; but also good for reducing resistance, reaching consensus and turning small victories into big ones. In practice, China started from local places to regions and from easier tasks to more difficult ones. For instance, pilot reforms were introduced in a few special economic zones (SEZs) in Shenzhen, Zhuhai, Shantou and Nanhai at the early stage of reform, and then reform was extended to 14 open coastal cities such as Xiamen, Ningbo, Qingdao and Dalian, and then a set of strategies were implemented such as letting the eastern region develop first, developing the west, revitalizing the northeast and facilitating the rise of the central region, and finally reform was extended to every corner of the nation. Another example is that, in order for reform to make breakthroughs, China initially carried out reform in rural areas where there were fewer barriers, and then extended reform to urban districts where there were more difficulties. In this way, it managed to consolidate the progress made in the early years of reform into more complex areas.

Second, China adheres to the idea of grasping the principle of contradictions and giving priority to important matters. Contradictions are either primary or secondary; likewise, some needs are urgent, while others are not. Since its inception, China's reform and opening up has emphasized grasping the principle of contradictions and focused on key links and important fields related to people's urgent needs. A slight move in one area may affect the whole situation; forge momentum and initiate a trend can move the whole situation forward. Before average per capita incomes reached a middle level, reform of the economic system was fundamental in China's reform, due to the fact that, during this period, economic development was the primary contradiction; and improving average per capita incomes was the priority, while the need for social construction and cultural development could be deferred. During the new period when GDP per capita exceeds US$6,000, the principal contradictions are being tackled in terms of reforming the administrative system and transforming government functions, improving general development by streamlining administration, delegating power to lower levels and conducting reform of the government. Meanwhile, as economic development rises, people are becoming more concerned with issues such as a better education, higher incomes, a fairer society and cleaner air. Consequently, reform must focus on these problems in order to form a social consensus and boost confidence in the reform process.

Third, China adheres to the idea that persistent development is the absolute truth. Deng Xiaoping, China's chief architect of reform and opening up, once said: "It doesn't matter whether a cat is black or white so long as it can catch mice." This means we should break the bondage of conventions and taboos, persist in starting from reality, free the mind, seek truth from facts, keep pace with the times and ensure that all policies are practical and useful. The 'cat theory' has saved China from ridiculous, far-left thoughts such as 'preferring socialist weeds to capitalist seedlings' and 'the poorer, the prouder', and has brought back common sense, promoted instrumental reason again, and avoided meaningless political arguments and irrational economic mistakes. In practice, Deng Xiaoping proposed 'three beneficials' as the criteria for judging the soundness of polices: whether we should adopt a certain reforming measure depends on whether it is 'beneficial to improvements in productivity, comprehensive national strength and living standards'. So long as any policy meets the criteria, we should 'make a bold attempt without argument and make corrections if the policy turns out bad'. The 'three beneficials' criteria have successfully handled the relationship between cognition and practice in the process of reform and opening up, and as a result thinking on reform has become clear. In light of this, China boldly absorbs and learns from the success of western countries in developing a market economy and introducing ways and approaches that are beneficial to economic development, such as the shareholding system, stock markets and financial derivatives. This mentality speeds up the unleashing of economic potential.

Fourth, China adheres to the idea of the coexistence of multiple elements.

Factors such as weak foundations, large scale and rapid transformation highlight the diversity of China's economy and society. Therefore, adherence to the coexistence of multiple elements fits the reality of reform. China takes 'the dominance of public ownership and co-development of diverse types of ownership' as the basic economic system, reflecting the characteristic of a mixed economy with multiple elements coexisting. China takes 'the dominance of distribution according to work and the co-existence of diverse distribution methods' as the distribution principle that fits well with the diversity of production and operation patterns, safeguards workers' status in distribution to a certain degree and stimulates the functions of many production elements, such as capital, land and technology. Since China was starting at a low point before its economy took off, with a severe shortage of resources such as capital and technology, the distribution system with multiple elements coexisting met the needs of economic development. The basic political system that 'multiple parties cooperate under the CPC's leadership' also reflects the coexistence of multiple elements. This political system can expand the ruling foundation as broadly as possible, and is good not only for integrating interests extensively, but also for improving the elasticity and stability of the political structure.

4.1.2 Taking economic system reform as the key point

The core of economic system reform is to properly handle the relationship of the government and the market. We should let the market play a decisive role in distributing resources, constantly perfect the modern market system and at the same time let the government play a role in macro regulation, public services, market supervision and so on, so as to boost productivity and optimize the distribution of production factors such as labor, knowledge, technology, management and capital.

First, China has been gradually removing system-related barriers and facilitating the flow of the labor force. The release of a demographic dividend is a key factor contributing to China's continuous rapid economic growth and is a crucial step of economic reform to perfect the market mechanism allowing the labor force to flow freely. China's traditional economic sector, agriculture, has an almost an inexhaustible labor supply. The process of the labor force moving to modern economic sectors is also the process of improving marginal productivity. In order to encourage surplus rural workers to move to non-agricultural industries, China has scrapped the food rationing system and job assignment system for university graduates. It has built the labor market, and tried to ensure the freedom for employees to choose jobs and for enterprises to choose employees. Coupled with this measure, China has been promoting the reform of the household registration system; gradually lifting the limits imposed on the rural population settling in cities, promoting the 'citizenization' of rural migrant workers; gradually perfecting the territorial social security system; pushing the marketization of real estate and seeking ways to construct a housing security system. All these measures have enhanced the flow of the labor force, largely released the demographic dividend, and promoted domestic production and consumption.

Second, China has been advancing the reform of enterprises and has allowed enterprises to play a principal role in developing the economy. Enterprises are the entities that compete in the market. The central link of China's economic reform chain is the reform of enterprises. In the 1980s, the government encouraged the development of township enterprises. The 1990s witnessed SOE reform, which involved the sound management of large enterprises while relaxing control over small ones. After 2000 came investment system reform. A series of reforms were made to enhance the power of public and non-public enterprises and incentivize them to develop freely according to market laws. Through a series of reforms of systems such as the property rights protection system, price system and circulation system, the Chinese government has been striving to create a benign market environment that allows all investors to compete fairly and in an orderly manner. With enterprises becoming participants of market competition and factor distribution, production efficiency of the whole of society has been greatly improved. At the end of 2012, China had 8,287,000 enterprises, including 550,000 state-owned or collective-owned enterprises, 6,550,000 private enterprises and 210,000 enterprises from overseas, Hong Kong, Macau and Taiwan. The non-public economy plays a key role and infuses unremitting vigor into the development of the national economy. Meanwhile, enterprises get to play a principal role in social innovation. In 2012, mega enterprises invested Rmb720bn in research and development, employed 2,246,000 researchers and applied for 490,000 patents, driving industrial technology to innovate and upgrade continuously.

Third, China has been constructing a market system that is open to the world and fully utilizes its comparative advantages to drive economic development. The Chinese economy has taken the initiative to enter the global market, participate in the global labor division system, actively attract foreign investment, encourage exports, and support and push forward trade liberalization. For example, China is building 16 free trade zones (FTZs) in collaboration with 29 countries and districts across five continents, and 10 of the 16 zones have already had their agreements signed and are now in operation. The signed free trade agreements include those with Asean, Singapore, Pakistan, New Zealand and Chile.[1] In addition, construction of China (Shanghai) Pilot FTZ shows that China will further open up its economy, in sectors such as finance and shipping, and look to higher-level free trade rules, such as pre-establishment national treatment and the negative list. The open market system has not only brought China many trading opportunities but also considerable investment, state-of-the-art technology and cutting-edge management. China has a comparative advantage in terms of the quality and price of the labor force. They have been fully utilized, making China globally competitive in the manufacture of labor-intensive products. Since reform and opening up, China's foreign trade growth rate has far exceeded the world average. The value of China's imports and exports accounted for 1% of world trade in the early 1980s, before rising to 8.8% in 2012. Foreign direct investment stood at US$115bn in 2012, of which US$77.2bn comprised non-financial direct investment, placing it among the top five in the world.[2]

Fourth, China has been constructing a financial decentralization system with Chinese characteristics to stimulate the enthusiasm of local governments in a developing economy. Although China is a unitary state, the decentralization of power in finance is obvious. Scholars such as Qian Yingyi call it 'fiscal federalism'. According to the system of tax distribution, central and local governments 'eat from separate kitchens'. The construction of dual tax systems, national and local, divides all national taxes between the central and local governments. There are three types of tax: central, local and shared. Local tax includes sales tax, local enterprise income tax, individual income tax and urban land-use tax. These taxes are closely tied to the level of local economic development. In order to expand the resources at their disposal, local governments have a strong desire to broaden the tax base, so they spare no effort in attracting investment and building industrial areas with a view to promoting local economic development. Competition among local governments over economic scale and economic growth rate has led to rapid economic growth nationwide and the improvement of many things such as industrial support and public services.

---

[1] China FTA Network, http://fta.mofcom.gov.cn

[2] Integrating the statistics of the EIU and of Xinhua News Agency. *Report Predicts China to Be a Net Capital Exporter in 2017*, www.yicai.com/news/2013/04/2621481.html. *Our Non-financial Outbound Direct Investment Reached US$77.22bn in 2012*, news.xinhuanet.com/fortune/2013-01/16/c_114392316

The achievements of China's reform and opening up have attracted worldwide attention, but many lessons have been learned the hard way. For example, the problems of imbalance, lack of coordination and unsustainability are evident, and there is a large income gap between urban and rural residents. The most prominent problem is that the reforms of the political, social, cultural and ecological systems have failed to catch up with economic system reform, resulting in vested interest groups trying to impede reforms; in particular, the slowness in introducing checks and balances, and anti-monopolistic and anti-corruption rules has obviously hindered China's modernization. Of course, the central government has come to realize the importance of 'top-level design', i.e. taking the reforms as a system in which different reforms affect each other, building a scientific framework on the top layer of the system, and making sure that the different elements of reform and innovation harmonize, match and promote one other. The third plenary session of the 18th central committee of the CPC proposed to emphasize the systematicity, wholeness and coherence of reform and set up 'a group of central leaders for comprehensively deepening reform' that takes charge of the overall design, planning, coordination, advancement and supervision of the reform.

4.2 Taking development as the key to solving all problems

In the opinion of the Chinese government, development means adhering to taking economic construction as the center; to comprehensively pushing forward the construction of the economy, politics, culture, society and ecological civilization; it also means promoting scientific development, and accelerating the production of social wealth and improving people's living standards.

4.2.1 Development is of overriding importance

In light of historical experience, Deng Xiaoping reemphasized the significance of developing social productivity. In 1992, he came up with the famous thesis 'development is of overriding importance', taking development as the central task and the very basis upon which to solve all problems confronting China. There are four reasons for him thinking in this way. First, developing productivity is the fundamental task of socialism. Whether socialism with Chinese characteristics can constantly consolidate and develop and whether it is superior depend on whether productivity can increase at a faster rate than under capitalism. Second, the importance of development is a profound lesson learned from the socialism practiced and experienced at home and abroad. During the 20-odd years before reform and opening up, China's socialist construction was not satisfactory. An important factor was our failure, for a relatively long time, to really take the development of productivity as the fundamental task of socialist construction. Socialism could by no means build on poverty and low levels of productivity for long. The key for China to solving its problems is to develop itself. This is the most important conclusion drawn from the experience and lessons of socialist construction at home and abroad through scientific analysis. Third, we rely on development to solve the principal contradictions of our society. China remains at the preliminary stage of socialism where the public's growing material and cultural needs and the backward state of social productivity constitute the principal social contradiction. And the contradiction can only be settled through the development of productivity. Fourth, development and peace are themes of the present era. As a socialist nation, China plays a role in protecting peace and stability and acts as an important contributing factor to the development of peaceful power. China's development is becoming a new force that propels the global economy. Adherence to development is of overriding importance. It requires settling the problems emerging in the process of development by looking to the future, with optimistic thoughts and developing methods, and continuously carrying forward the socialist cause with Chinese characteristics.

4.2.2 A summary of the fundamental experiences of China's economic development

The most fundamental reason for the rapidity with which the Chinese economy develops is that we base our choice of the route and method of development on the characteristics of China's national circumstances and its comparative advantages. 'A large population and a weak economic foundation' are the chief characteristics of China's national circumstances. Abundant labor resources and a huge domestic market are its most important comparative advantages. Consequently, China has decided to focus first on labor-intensive industries; then gradually to upgrade them into capital-intensive and high-tech-intensive industries and push agriculture, manufacturing and service industries forward in a coordinated fashion.

Specifically, first, we emphasize the fundamental position of agriculture. We should deeply understand the saying 'no agriculture, no stability', and relentlessly strengthen the fundamental position of this sector. There are two old sayings in China: 'Food is as important as heaven for the people' and 'With food in hand, there is no need to panic'. Food is of paramount importance and bound up in the development of the whole nation. China always persists in putting work concerning agriculture, the countryside and farmers at the top of its development agenda. From 'fixing farm output quotas for each household', lifting control over the 'food circulation system', 'foregoing agricultural tax', 'subsidizing farmers for growing grain' up to 'constructing a new socialist countryside', China has taken a raft of measures to boost agricultural production, as well as farmers' incomes and rural development. The heart of all the measures is to protect farmers' interests and stimulate their enthusiasm for production, especially of grain. China is home to 1,826m mu (487,000 square miles) of arable land, taking up 7% of the world's total. Although this is equivalent to 1.4 mu per capita, less than half of the world average, China has managed to feed 20% of the world's population. It has reaped good harvests of grain for 10 years in succession, having completely solved the challenge of feeding 1.3bn people and thus laid a solid foundation for the healthy development of its economy.

Second, we emphasize the leading part that industry plays. We deeply understand the logic of 'no industry, no affluence', and constantly enhance industry's leading role. Industry has far more value added than agriculture. China has chosen the industrial development route and development programs after carefully considering its own comparative advantages. It boasts abundant labor resources, a relatively fertile and vast land, and rich natural resources. What China lacks is capital, technology and management talent. Therefore, the mode China has adopted for its industrial development is 'walking on two legs'.

The first leg walks on the road of independence and self-reliance, prioritizing the development of industry by relying on its own strength. China started from 'household workshops', then developed 'township enterprises' and finally is now developing collectively-owned, state-owned and privately-owned enterprises. Industrial development started with the handicrafts, textiles and other light industries; then it moved to develop the heavy chemical and advanced manufacturing industries; and now it is developing the high and new technology industry. In the process of industrialization, China has emphasized the development of the individual economy and small and medium-sized scientific and technological enterprises by supporting them with privileged fiscal and financial policies. After several decades of development, China has built an independent and quite complete industrial system. In the next phase, it will choose seven strategic and emerging industries – energy conservation and environmental protection, the new generation of information technology, biology, high-end equipment manufacturing, new energy, new materials and new energy vehicles – and focus on developing them, with a view to upgrading the industrial structure and transforming the economic development mode.

The second leg walks on the road of opening up to the world. Despite the reality that its basic conditions were very awkward, China grasped the opportunity at a time when global manufacturers were starting to establish plants overseas by making great efforts to attract foreign investment, technology and management talent. The means of opening up included setting up SEZs, opening coastal, riparian and border cities, economic and technological development zones (ETDZs), bonded areas and free trade areas. The construction of these open districts highlighted the guideline 'giving priority to industry, and attracting foreign investment and expertise', and adopted the policy of 'befriending and favoring businessmen, and treating them well'. The detailed policies encompassed the sayings 'three supplied and one compensation' (processing with supplied materials, processing according to supplied samples, assembling parts supplied by clients and compensation trade), and 'two exemptions and three halves' (two-year income tax exemption and three-year income tax 50% reduction). These policies granted special privileges to foreign businessmen and facilitated the progression of industrialization, with urbanization, informatization and agricultural modernization developing simultaneously.

Third, we brought into full play the inner vigor of the market economy. We should deeply understand 'no commerce, no vigor' and constantly enhance the inner vigor of the market economy. Commodity circulation is the lubricant and stimulant of the market economy. Commercial development not only promotes industrial development and satisfies people's needs, but can also stabilize prices and promote employment. China developed a commercial service industry by starting from supporting individual traders and peddlers who were also called 'street vendors'. They moved around streets to sell goods. The individual economy not only stimulated commodity circulation but also partly solved the employment issue for many people. Market transactions became more active with each passing day. The variety of commodities multiplied. New business models sprang up one after another such as department stores, supermarkets, famous brand franchises, specialty shops and online supermarkets. In this new era, ecommerce flourished. A number of famous Chinese internet companies stand out, such as Alibaba, Taobao Net, Dangdang Net and Jingdong Mall, to name just a few. Online commodity transactions are increasing exponentially. In 2012, the total value of China's online retail market reached Rmb1,320.5bn, increasing by 65.7%, year-on-year, and accounting for 6.3% of total retail sales of consumer goods. Meanwhile, China's large, comprehensive trading markets and specialized trading markets have prospered. For example, the Canton Fair, founded in 1957 and held twice a year, is a large-scale event that exerts great influence. In addition, Yiwu small commodities market in Zhejiang province, which was founded in 1982, today occupies an area of more than 2.6m square meters. It has more than 50,000 stores, 200,000 employees and 200,000 customers daily, and encompasses 43 industries, 1,900 types of commodity and 1,700,000 different commodities. It is the world's leading small commodity market.

Fourth, we took a people-centered and sustainable development approach. The third plenary session of the 16th central committee of the CPC proposed for the first time a 'scientific outlook on development'. Superficially, this proposal was caused directly by the spread of SARS (severe acute respiratory syndrome) in the spring of 2003. But the deeper cause was that the imbalance, inequality and unsustainability of China's economic development mode that had restrained the economy from developing continuously. The core of scientific outlook on development is to put people first; and the basic requirement is to develop comprehensively and in a coordinated and sustainable way; the fundamental method is to make overall planning by giving due consideration to the interests of all parties concerned in society, which involves coordinating urban and rural development; regional development; economic and social development; the development of people and nature; and domestic development and opening up.

People-orientation runs through China's reform and development. It is in the interest of the public that we implement reform and pursue economic growth. If the dividends of reform or the fruits of development fail to benefit the people, then reform will lose steam; development will lose meaning; a stable environment will be left unprotected and the construction of a harmonious society will lose public support.

How to put people first when we pursue development? We have to realize, protect and enlarge the fundamental interests of the overwhelming majority of people. We must always take this purpose as the starting point and basis for our policies. We also have to respect people's principal position, give free rein to their creative spirit, protect their interests, take the road of common

Chapter 4

prosperity and facilitate their all-round development. We have to develop for the sake of the people, rely on them and let them share the fruits of our development. To put it more specifically, China's economic construction not only stresses creating more material wealth, sometimes referred to as 'making the cake big', but also emphasizes improving living standards, raising the ratio of individual incomes in national revenue distribution and the ratio of workers' pay in preliminary distribution ('dividing the cake rationally'). Meanwhile, the Chinese government is paying more and more attention to social construction, prioritizing people's livelihoods, accelerating the development of social undertakings concerning science and technology, education, culture, sanitation and sports, continually satisfying people's demands for spirituality, health and safety, and combining the acceleration of economic development with the promotion of social progress.

How, then, to develop in a comprehensive, well-balanced and sustainable way? We have to promote the all-round construction of the economy, politics, culture, society and ecological civilization, coordinate different chains and aspects of modernization, and push the whole of society on to a road of civilized development with increased production, affluence and a perfect ecological environment. The key lies in transforming the mode of economic development, basing economic development on structural optimization and quality improvement; discarding the belief that GDP is the most important measure; solving the problems of overlapping industrial structures in different geographical areas, a failure to invest in technology and productivity gains, and an over-emphasis on quantity rather than quality by changing the systems relating to tax, finance and investment. In order to realize sustainable development, China is now endeavoring to develop an intensive economy, developing new industries, by adjusting the industrial structure; settling the problem of excess production capacity; and reducing the prevalence of industries characterized by high energy consumption, pollution and high emissions. For the purpose of saving resources and protecting the environment, China is now vigorously developing a recycling economy, promoting green production and civilized consumption in society. It is also cultivating a policy environment and a development mechanism, both of which are favorable to low input, high output and recyclability, and constructing a conservation-minded society in an all-round way. China is also drawing on the advancements of science and technology to shore up its practices concerning energy conservation and emission reduction.

4.3 Stability is a precondition for reform and development

Instead of adopting shock therapy in an attempt to attain the final objective in one step, China's reform has taken a progressive approach, moving forward in small, fast yet continuous steps to avoid shocking society too much. Stable politics and a steady social situation create beneficial conditions for continuing and deepening reform. Stability means maintaining good order for the development of politics, the economy and society. Without a stable political, economic and social environment, no sound reforming measure can be put into practice. Therefore, China's ruling party and government take stability as the 'primary task' for leaders at all levels and require them to handle competently the subtle relationships between reform, development and stability. They should adhere to the order from 'reform to development and then to stability', putting reform first when thinking about problems; they should adhere to the order from 'stability to development and then to reform', putting stability first when dealing with societal problems. To be more specific, the practices of China's ruling party and government to promote stability are described below.

4.3.1 They strengthen the leadership of the CPC and build an efficient and effective government of action

The CPC is not only the founder of the new Chinese government but also the leader of the great task of reform, opening up and modernization. It has built a powerful government and taken on the heavy historical responsibility of transforming China from an impoverished agricultural country into a modernized one. Its outstanding ability to integrate resources, manage society and solve contradictions has enabled it to pass many tests and provide a powerful political guarantee for China's economic take-off and social stability. Because the CPC is appointed by the constitution as the ruling party, it has a long-term responsibility for China's development, which motivates it to take particular care about the long-term effects of its policies. Therefore, the CPC has a natural advantage in terms of ensuring the continuity of policies. 'Who has public support, rules; who loses public support, fails.'

How can the party and the government earn public support? First, they promote democracy and ensure that people's democratic rights are exercised. The essence of democracy is to let the people be the masters. The means and form for conducting democracy have to be decided by the people with consideration of the country's history and culture and of the specific period of development. Then, they perfected the legal system, effectively protecting people's rights and maintaining social order and stability. Next, they are good at unifying all possible strengths and motivating all possible active elements, especially the enthusiasm of intellectuals. As Mao Zedong said: "We should increase the number of people who agree with us and decrease the number of people who are against us." Finally, the party and government are good at recognizing, grasping and making good use of opportunities. Opportunities are fleeting. They grasp the opportunities to develop the country based on their knowledge of the national situation and global trends.

4.3.2 They improve government macro regulation while giving full play to the role of the market

The government regulates the market and the market, in turn, guides enterprises. This is an important system that helps to maintain the rapid development of China's economy and stabilizes the economy and society. For a developing economy, it is both important and necessary for the government to use economic, legal and administrative tools to regulate economic activities. Government regulation of the economy should guarantee these four aspects: 'economic growth', 'basic price stability', 'full employment in society' and 'a basic balance of international payments'. Meanwhile, the government should give full play to the fundamental and guiding roles of the market price mechanism, supply-demand mechanism and competition mechanism in the distribution of social resources and enterprises' activities. In general, the government should not directly interfere in the microeconomic activities of enterprises, but instead should regulate and influence the market through financial and monetary policies and let the market price mechanism guide the activities of enterprises; this way, it can achieve the objectives of economic and social development. This is a significant way to make the economy more robust and maintain economic stability. In order to give full play to the role of the market, the Chinese government has passed a series of rules and laws to maintain normal market order, such as *The Anti-unjust Competition Law*, *The Price Law* and *The Patent Law*, and has also made special policies (two '36-point guidelines on non-public sectors') to encourage the growth of the non-public economy, so as to create a systematic environment for the public and non-public economy to compete fairly.

4.3.3 They guarantee and improve people's livelihoods, reform the income distribution system and promote common prosperity

China has come to realize that social policies produce clear economic effects. Improving people's livelihoods is not only necessary for stabilizing society, but also conducive to turning an investment-driven economy into a consumption-driven one. China takes four typical measures to solve problems related to people's livelihoods. First, it emphasizes that education is the foundation of people's livelihoods and endeavors to realize educational equality, especially the equalization of quality education resources. Second, it emphasizes that employment is the basis of people's livelihoods and endeavors to bring about full employment and keep unemployment below 4.5%. Third, China emphasizes that social security is the safety valve of people's livelihoods and endeavors to build a social security system that equally covers every person, urban or rural, and that includes provision for the elderly, the unemployed and healthcare. Fourth, China emphasizes that income distribution is the source of people's livelihoods and endeavors to optimize the combination of 'efficiency and fairness' in the process of income distribution.

The government has the responsibility to let all people enjoy the achievements of economic development; and the responsibility to prevent the income gap from widening too much. If it fails, the poor will start to hate the rich, undermining social harmony and stability. How should we view the income gap? First, we should make sure that there are appropriate gaps in income distribution and that these gaps spur improvements in efficiency; denial of the income gap will suffocate society's development momentum and vitality. Second, we should control the income gap to a range that is still bearable by society and 'establish a floor, but not a ceiling'. Third, we should strive to realize common prosperity, always following the principle of 'raising the low, expanding the middle, adjusting the high and punishing the illegal'; in other words, raising incomes that are too low, expanding the number of people with middle incomes, adjusting incomes that are too high and punishing those whose income is earned through illegal means. This way, we will be able to gradually build an oval-shaped class structure.

China persists in organically combining the intensity of reform, development speed and endurance of society, in order to keep the economy growing and society stable. However, some lessons have been learned the hard way relating to the maintenance of social stability. In particular, the number of mass incidents has been going up over recent years; the costs of 'maintaining stability' (keep society in good order) are rising; and the credibility of the government is deteriorating. These problems are becoming rampant. We feel that, in order to better maintain social stability, we must adhere to the principle of openness, fairness and justice. Openness enhances political honesty; fairness and justice win public support. Second, we should supervise government officials, determinedly oppose and punish all kinds of slackness, passiveness and corruption, 'shackle power within the cage of the system', combat administrative corruption by reinforcing the law; obviate political corruption by reforming the system; and strengthen the credibility of the government by being honest and upright. Third, we should protect the fundamental and legal rights of the majority of people, construct effective channels to express the real needs of most people, promote socialist democracy and prevent people with power and wealth from hijacking policies.

China's reform has no perfect tense, only a progressive tense. The Chinese people are still continuously searching for, and perfecting a development method that best suits the country. The development method of each country obviously has its own specific national features and it benefits from learning from other countries. All successful development methods must have an open-ended and inclusive theory and must emphasize the outcome, not the form. 'The Chinese method' is both a crystallization of Chinese wisdom and a blending of the fruits of different civilizations brought in by opening up. China has never refused to learn from the successful experiences of the outside world; and has never imposed its own systems on other nations. The Chinese method and its systems are not perfect, and have inherent shortcomings, just as with any other method or system, but the shortcomings are those that we encounter in the process of growth and those that inevitably occurred in the progress of history. This reflects the analogy drawn by Xi Jinping, president of China: "Only the wearer knows whether the shoes fit his feet or not." There is no universally applicable method of development; nor is there any development method that stays unchanged. Every country should choose a suitable development method in accordance with its own specific national conditions.

Chapter 5

Why were Development Zones Created as Part of Reform and Opening Up?

Over the past 30 years, in the process of reform and opening up and as showcases for all regions to develop an export-oriented economy, development zones have served as important linkages in China's value chain, performing radiating, showcasing and guiding functions. Development zones have become a great force, propelling their regional economies. As 'pilot areas' and 'pace-setters' of reform and opening up, and with the support of special and favorable policies, development zones have undertaken systematic innovations and have constantly experimented with different kinds of reform and made explorations in terms of introducing foreign investment, technology and management, conducting foreign trade, and adjusting industrial structure. In this way, they have accumulated a very rich experience of development.

5.1 The types and growth of development zones

China's economic development zones have evolved over nearly 35 years, starting from the year when Dalian ETDZ was officially founded. These zones include high and new technology development zones (HNTDZs), economic and technological development zones (ETDZs), export processing zones (EPZs), bonded zones, border economic cooperation zones, tourism development zones and ecological economic zones. They can be found all over the nation.

First, ETDZs are located in those parts of China that are open to the world. Relatively small areas in open cities are designated as such zones; financial strength is concentrated there to build the complete infrastructure needed to create an investment environment that meets international standards. Through attracting foreign investment, a modern industrial structure focused on new and high technology industry is formed. The zones have become important districts for the cities where they are located and for neighboring districts to develop foreign trade. Up to the end of 2013, the State Council permitted the construction of more than 200 economic development zones, such as Dalian ETDZ, Qinhuangdao ETDZ and Qingdao ETDZ; and the zones that follow the policies of ETDZs, such as Suzhou Industrial Park, Jinqiao Export Processing Zone (Shanghai), Daxie ETDZ (Ningbo), Haicang Investment Zone (Xiamen) and Yangpu Development Zone (Hainan).

Second, the purpose of setting up HNTDZs is to create a friendly environment for the industrialization of high and new technologies. By carrying out preferential policies concerning high technologies such as a reduction or exemption of tax and a sound system that supports these policies, the zones aim to create an industry agglomeration advantage and an industrialization environment that can attract and pull together talent, technology and capital, and can accelerate the transfer of new and high technologies into industrialization. Since the government authorized the 'torch program' in 1988, high and new technology development zones have developed rapidly, making outstanding contributions to the industrialization of high and new technology. Up to the end of 2013, the government had set up 105 HNTDZs, such as Zhongguancun Science and Technology Park, Donghu New Technology Industry Development Zone (Wuhan), Chengdu HNTDZ and Binhai HNTDZ (Tianjin).

Third, bonded zones are areas that are permitted by the State Council to carry out international trade and bonded business, similar to the free trade zones in countries where foreign businessmen are allowed to invest and carry out international trade, bonded warehousing and export processing. Since December 30, 2012, China's 15 bonded zones have all been in operation such as Waigaoqiao Bonded Zone (Shanghai), Shantou Bonded Zone, Haikou Bonded Zone and Xiangyu Bonded Zone (Xiamen). They have become interfaces between the Chinese and global economies.

Fourth, border economic cooperation zones are those areas in China where open border cities carry out border trade and export processing. The opening of border trade was a crucial strand of the opening up of central and western China. Since 1992, the State Council has approved 15 border economic cooperation zones and they have played a positive role in boosting economic trade and furthering good relations between China and neighboring countries and regions and in developing the economy of areas inhabited by Chinese minority nationalities. At the end of 2013, there were 15 national-level border economic cooperation zones, including ones in Heihe, Huichun, Manzhouli, Ruili and Hekou.

Fifth, the purpose of setting up EPZs is to promote the development of processing trade, standardize the management of processing trade, concentrate the location of processing trade factories, create a relaxed business environment for enterprises and encourage the expansion of exports. On April 27, 2000, the State Council officially approved the establishment of EPZs under the supervision of customs. To facilitate operation, the government has located EPZs in established development zones and chosen certain districts for pilot study. At the end of 2013, there were 63 national-level EPZs, including ones in Dalian, Tianjin, Kunshan, Yantai, Xiamen and Jinqiao. In addition, in the course of reform and opening up, China has set up 12 comprehensive reform-supportive pilot areas.

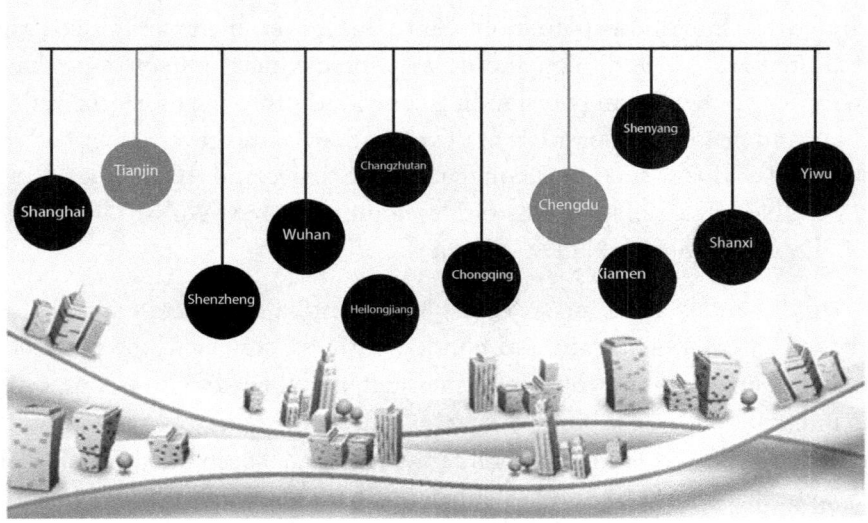

(Created by Zhang Xuan, journalist of Xinhua News Agency)

5.2 The practices and features of China's construction of development zones

5.2.1 The developmental process of development zones

China's development zones have been in existence for 30 years. The development process is as follows.

The initial period (1980-1990) Since 1980, the government has set up SEZs in Shenzhen, Zhuhai, Shantou and Xiamen. In 1984, the State

Council permitted the founding of 10 ETDZs in Dalian, Qinhuangdao, Yantai, Qingdao, Ningbo, Guangzhou, Zhanjiang, Tianjin, Lianyungang and Nantong. By the end of the 1980s, another four ETDZs had been approved, in Fuzhou, Minhang (Shanghai), Hongqiao (Shanghai) and Caohejing. This gave a total of 14 national ETDZs. In this period, the development zones relied mainly on favorable government policies and had formed an investment environment that was attractive for foreign investment. They had also accumulated some initial capital, technology, information and experience in the management of talent, and established a number of Taiwan-invested, cooperative and sole-investor enterprises. Initially, they made use of these favorable policies and found a mode of infrastructure construction with Chinese characteristics; every zone built infrastructure in a certain area that was suitable for foreign investment. The zones also clarified their development direction. Through bold practice and mutual learning, the zones had developed a common understanding. Based on a development tenet known as 'four windows' – technology window, management window, knowledge window and foreign policy window – the zones made a more practical and more accurate development guideline known as 'three mainlys' – 'mainly developing industries, mainly using foreign investment and mainly developing exports to earn foreign exchange'. During this period, the scale of the zones was smaller and the form was simple. Enterprises in the zones boasted little technology and were mainly labor-intensive. Technology transfer seldom happened. Light industries such as apparel and food and beverages dominated the industrial structure. Cooperation between enterprises rarely occurred. The development zones were mostly 'solitary islands', far away from the mother cities and relatively closed.

The rapid growth period (1991-1997) In the 1990s, while the strategy to develop an export-oriented economy was being carried out rapidly in coastal districts, especially after Deng Xiaoping made his 'southern tour speeches' in 1992 that affirmed the policy to implement a market economy and reform and open up, the development zones experienced a flowering period. They extended from coastal regions to border and riparian regions and even to inland provincial capitals. The construction of development zones surged across the whole nation. During this period, China's HNTDZs were deepening reform and developing rapidly in the favorable environment created by the expansion of the opening-up policy. According to incomplete statistics, at the end of 1996, there were 32 national ETDZs, 52 national HNTDZs, 11 national tourism development zones and 13 bonded zones that were all approved by the General Administration of Customs. Altogether, there were more than 100 national development zones, more than 400 provincial development zones and almost 10,000 development zones above township level. The development zones were diverse as well as numerous. For example, there were industrial zones, free port zones, bonded zones, tourism zones and high-tech industrial parks. The industrial structure of development zones, which used to be dominated by simple light industry, had diversified, and had become inhabited by industries such as automobiles, electronics, computer and information processing equipment, chemicals and chemical engineering, and equipment manufacturing.

The perfection period (1997-present) Since 1999, in order to correct the unbalanced development of different regions, the central government has been pursuing a strategy of developing the west. It authorized the provincial capitals in central and western regions to set up development zones. The State Council approved 11 national ETDZs in Hefei, Xi'an, Zhengzhou, Chengdu, Changsha, Kunming, Guiyang, Nanchang, Shihezi, Hohhot and Xining in 2000, and, in the following year, a further four national ETDZs were added in Nanning, Taiyuan, Yinchuan and Lhasa. In addition, Suzhou Industrial Park, Jinqiao EPZ (Shanghai), Haicang Investment Zone (Xiamen), Daxie Economic Development Zone (Ningbo) and Yangpu Development Zone (Hainan) began to enjoy the policies of national development zones. Meanwhile, in 2000, the State Council officially gave approval to the establishment of EPZs and decided to initially establish 15 pilot zones. Later, in 2002 and 2003 respectively, 10 and 13 EPZs were added to the list, making a total of 38. At the end of 2003, there were 195 national development zones across the country, including five SEZs, 54 ETDZs, 54 NTDZs, 38 export processing zones, 15 bonded zones, 14 border economic cooperation zones, 11 tourism zones and four Taiwanese investment zones.

Take a look at the overall development of China's development zones and we can see that they encompass SEZs, coastal open cities, coastal ETDZs, coastal and inland ETDZs, and HTDZs. The development process started with 'dots' (choosing some places) and then developed to 'lines' (linking those places to form a bigger area) and finally formed 'planes' (bringing them together to form a large region). The transition from planned economy to market economy required the establishment of ETDZs; it also required us to attract more foreign direct investment, promote exports and take part in the international division of labor. The development of ETDZs has helped to build up important momentum for the progress of technology, the adjustment of industrial structure and fast economic growth. The planning, construction, development speed, and scale and quality of development zones have all become vital factors affecting the pace of urbanization.

5.2.2 The practices and features of China's construction of development zones

Over the past 30 years or so, development zones have placed an emphasis on exploiting their own advantages associated with policies, systems, locations and talent, and constantly encouraged reform and innovation with an open and learning attitude, a pioneering spirit and consideration of the real circumstances. Development zones have been innovative in implementing a system of paying for land use and promoting reform of the social security system. They have actively searched for an efficient management system and attempted implementing a 'leader-employment system'.

a. Innovation of governmental administration theories

In order to win the approval of investors and adapt to the needs of a market economy, the various development zones in China have, from the beginning, laid special emphasis on the innovation of management theories. This is embodied in the following aspects.

First, development zones strive to integrate with international practices and follow the new management theory of 'service-oriented government'. For example, Suzhou Industrial Park has absorbed the essence of Singapore's pro-business public management theory. To follow pro-business thought means that the park administration should put services for clients at the top of its agenda; implement pro-business thought in its attitude and values while attracting business and investment and conducting daily management services; help clients achieve a satisfactory rate of return to enjoy the services provided, while letting the park enjoy corresponding benefits so as to create a win-win situation. Pro-business thought does not regard the government as the real creator of wealth. Only if the government successfully provides an environment favorable to the development of industry and commerce and let enterprises have a higher rate of return than in any other country or district, can the government attract more quality investment and can the national economy grow rapidly.

Second, development zones at different levels have made very fruitful explorations in the area of administration by rule of law. The transformation of management thought from rule by men to the rule of law and the stress on the construction of systems and regulations have made the administrative management of national development zones more scientific than the traditional management style. With administrative management becoming more scientific, the risk expectation of investors has been greatly lowered. Besides, great progress has been achieved in terms of the transparency of law enforcement. The rise of transparency has lowered the cost of investment transactions, which in turn has further raised the rate of successful investment. Most national development zones are working to create a fair, open and just social and investment climate. It is because of the transformation of management theory that national development zones can become China's most attractive investment destination.

Third, in the process of planning, construction and development, development zones at every level all take 'putting people first' as the guideline. The management mode of 'putting people first' means taking people as the starting point and center in the process of management and carrying out management activities with the aim of stimulating public activeness, initiative and creativity and realizing common development of the people, zones and enterprises. Under the guidance of 'putting people first', development zones at different levels, especially those that function well, have changed the simple and crude management method under the planned economic system and now view people as the primary factor of economic development.

b. Support given by government policies and systematic innovation

China's development zones at all levels have made many beneficial attempts to improve the arrangement of government policies and innovate government functions.

First, the central government has introduced favorable policies to support development zones. For example, it provides enterprises in development zones free use of land and factory buildings; gives foreign-invested manufacturing enterprises a preferential income tax rate of 15%; grants favors to export products manufactured in development zones and some imported items with preferential tax policies; and offers a tax deduction or even exemption to high and new technological products made in those HNDTZs. With the benefit of these preferential policies, following the 'three mainly' development guideline – 'mainly developing industries, mainly using foreign investment and mainly developing exports to earn foreign exchange' – and taking into consideration their specific conditions, the development zones have gradually expanded their scale, improved production levels and moved toward modernization and integration. Government support for development zones with favorable policies enables the zones to accumulate capital and thus develop continuously.

Second, the central government has innovated all the systems of a market economy and helped development zones flourish. Development zones are the 'showcases' of China's opening up; 'pilot areas' of reform; and new growth points of regional economic development. Therefore, development zones have made a number of fruitful explorations about system innovation and tried to create an international investment environment, transform government functions, increase service consciousness and perfect all the systems within the frame of the market economy. Plenty of experiences concerning the government and entrepreneurs have been acknowledged and disseminated in the reform. Development zones have established the internal management system for administrative government departments characterized by balancing responsibility and power on the one hand and simplified institutions and high efficiency on the other. Through unceasing exploration and practice, the development zones in different regions have reformed their administrative system. Out of the 53 existing national development zones, 46 have adopted the administration mode of 'quasi-government'.

According to this mode, an administrative committee is appointed to represent the municipal government; economically, it mainly carries out its administrative functions at the corresponding level of government. The municipal party committee also appoints a working committee to development zones, but no people's congress or political consultative conference is set up; the municipal government empowers the administrative committee and allows it to exercise municipal-level power.

The administrative institutions of development zones have been freed from the practice of taking care of everything as they would have done under the planned economic system after the government's functions began to be defined mainly by the market economy. On the one hand, the administrative function is defined according to the administrative mode of 'small government, big society', in which the government's administrative function is greatly reduced. On the other hand, development zones place the focus of their own functions on creating the conditions necessary for the smooth running of enterprises, and predominantly on improving the investment environment by, say, constructing infrastructure, enhancing the living environment and improving the industrial environment. Development zones rarely get involved in public administration. Promoting investment, especially attracting business and investment, is the government's major function in terms of promoting economic development. Such a functional transformation has laid a solid foundation for streamlining government bodies, reducing the administrative burden of having to deal with different departments and achieving high efficiency.

Some of the functions that used to belong to the traditional management system (according to the principle of a market economy, those do not fit the category of governmental functions) are left to non-governmental agencies in society, such as inward investment and labor service companies. To sum up, the administrative system in China's development zones always retain the characteristics of simplicity, efficiency and correspondence between power and responsibility.

Third, a flexible mode of public administration has been developed. As the pilot areas of China's reform and opening up, immediately after they were founded, economic development zones broke from the shackles set by traditional systems by making bold innovations, and adopted new types of administrative system to ensure the realization of their special functions. At present, the administrative systems practiced by different economic development zones fall into three main types: government-dominated, government-enterprise combined and enterprise-dominated. Following the principle of simplicity, high efficiency and service-orientation, and being set up in line with local circumstances, these administrative systems are diversified, flexible and have shown some 'systemic effect'.

Some development zones adopt the mode of government-dominated administration. Generally speaking, provincial or municipal leaders create a leadership team responsible for coordinating significant decisions and problems concerning the zone, but not for handling specific matters. Everyday specific matters are left to the zone's administrative committee. In government-dominated development zones, the power wielded by the administrative committee is relatively great, which is good for the development of development zones at the initial stage, and for the coordination of all kinds of relations within the zones and for improving efficiency. Donghu High and New Zone (Shandong), Beijing Zhongguancun, Qingdao High-tech Park and Suzhou High and New Zone all adopt this type of management mode.

Some development zones adopt the government-enterprise-combined mode. The administrative committee and construction and development company bear their own separate names, but share the same staff and same offices. Performing both administrative and economic functions, the administration committee of the development zone is both manager and developer. Due to the fact that this mode is highly efficient and that it gives the administrators considerable freedom in the early stage of development, many development zones started with this mode, including Xi'an HNTDZ.

Some development zones adopt the enterprise-dominated mode. The construction and development company takes full charge of the daily operation of development zones. Usually, it is a non-profit service entity delivering government policies, offering comprehensive services such as providing land, capital, development conditions, information and advice on the administration of talent exchange, and creating an optimized environment in a limited area for entrepreneurs that have made significant high-tech achievements. Through these channels, they provide support to the development of high-tech enterprises and facilitate the realization of scientific and technological achievements. This mode has obvious advantages, such as a simple organization, clear definition of power and responsibilities, and large-scale development. However, due to the absence of administrative agencies, the development zone has no administrative functions concerning land appropriation, planning, examination and approval of programs, and transfer of personnel. Weak administrative coordination limits the development of zones in many aspects.

China's economy is now in a period of transition. The imperfections in a market economy show that the government still needs to assume some responsibilities in economic affairs. Against such a background, the management modes of China's development zones need to be diversified.

5.3 The achievements and experiences of development zones

5.3.1 The achievements of development zones

In the summer of 1986, Deng Xiaoping wrote the following inscription for Tianjin Economic Development Zone: "Development zones hold great expectations." After a period of 30 years, development zones have become the pioneers of China's reform and opening up and achieved a great deal for China's socialist construction and exploration.

First, the economy in development zones has benefited from scale and quality. During the 10th five-year plan, the regional GDP of the 54 national development zones increased by 34.51% annually on average, contributing more than 6.2% to national economic growth. At the end of the 10th five-year plan, the 54 national development zones had a gross production worth Rmb815.9bn, accounting for 4.49% of national GDP; gross industrial output was valued at Rmb2,337.7bn, a rise by 37.77% year on year during the period; industrial value added reached Rmb598.1bn, a growth of 35.24% annually during the period; tax revenue totaled Rmb121.9bn, representing an annual growth rate of 32.77%. The contribution made by national development zones to the economic growth of the cities where they are located was becoming more evident day by day, with the zones' gross production accounting for between 10% and 30% of that of the cities. Development zones became the growth pole of regional economic development. Upon entering the 11th five-year plan period, national development zones had maintained a robust economic growth trend. By concentrating production and planning prudently, national development zones have become regions with the highest efficiency in the use of land and energy. On average, every square kilometer of industrial land has generated Rmb1.3bn of industrial value added, Rmb5.3bn of total industrial output, Rmb275m of tax revenue and 8,000 jobs. The national development zones' energy consumption for every Rmb10,000 of industrial value added is about 25% of that of the whole nation; their water consumption for every Rmb10,000 of industrial value added is less than 9% of the national average. National development zones have found a new industrialization road that is highly scientific and technological, with good economic benefits and little pollution, and having nurtured the potential of its human resources.

Meanwhile, national development zones constantly optimize their industrial structure and extend their industrial chains step by step. As the effect of industrial agglomeration is becoming ever more evident, national development zones have become important elements of international industrial specialization and global market circulation. They have developed industrial agglomerations in sectors such as electronic information, transportation equipment, electronic equipment, biomedicine, chemicals, aviation and aerospace, and food and beverages. Nationally, these industries are growing particularly fast in development zones, and as a result the zones have become national centers of modern manufacturing. Modern service industries, such as logistics, software development, finance, insurance, consulting and intermediary services, have also developed in national development zones, and a competitive edge has already been secured in service sectors that support and promote efficiency and the use of technology in production.

Second, development zones make outstanding contributions to high and new technological industries. Most of the initial foreign investment projects in development zones were small or medium-sized labor-intensive enterprises; technology transfer was rare. As more large transnational corporations were attracted to China, the scale of foreign investment projects in development zones expanded quickly; and the technological content and quality of projects has also improved. These have not only brought in advanced technology, management experience, operation philosophy and knowledge about how to run corporations, but have also updated public understanding of production and turned out many high-quality technicians, managers and industrial workers. National development zones have attracted a group of high and new technological industries, such as electronic information, biotechnology, new materials, mechanical and electronic integration, aviation and aerospace, environmental protection and marine technology. In 2007, there were 4,039 government-recognized high and new technology enterprises above provincial level in the 54 national development zones, increasing by 23.21% year on year. The gross industrial output of high and new technological enterprises was valued at Rmb1,889.8bn in 2007, increasing 32.47% year on year, 2.19% higher than the total value of output generated by national development zones, and accounting for 49.2% of the total value of industrial production of these zones.

Third, development zones are 'spearheads' and a significant factor in the rise of central China and the development of the western region. Take 2007 as an example. The growth rates of the major economic indicators of development zones in central and western regions were all higher than those in the east. The 13 national development zones in the west grew at the fastest speed: the growth rates of regional gross value of production, total industrial value added, industrial output, tax revenue and utilized foreign investment (the major economic indicators in China) all exceeded 40%, far higher than the 20% average growth rate of the 54 national development zones. Most economic indicators of the 22 development zones in central and western regions have been one percentage point higher compared with the average of the 54 national development zones. The gap between development zones in the eastern, central and western regions is narrowing.

Fourth, development zones are the 'experimental fields' of modern urban construction. Economic development zones have advantages in developing the economy, utilizing foreign capital and raising money for urban construction. They also function to attract business and investment and act as incubators for new and high technologies. As a result, most development zones have developed substantially in terms of infrastructure construction and park environment. Let us consider Suzhou Industrial Park. It has developed in line with the requirements for new city zones, in that it is internationalized, modernized and landscaped. By learning from the successful experiences of advanced cities at home and abroad, it has innovated its concepts concerning the construction and development of new city zones and planned its 'indexing system' in a detailed and complete way. It has scientifically planned its urban development boundary, development degree and functional layout, emphasizing perspective, science and operability. It has made efforts to improve the standard of city-specific design, optimize the systems of urban construction, management and assessment, and build an urban resource utilization system that is both industrial park-specific and sustainable.

5.3.2 The experiences of development zones

Over the past 30 years of growth, development zones have always pursued the truth, respected facts, followed the inner logic and laws of economic development, explored with boldness, operated with courage, and accumulated precious nuggets of experience by learning from past successes and failures. The experiences they have garnered can be summed up as follows.

First, adherence to mental emancipation and seeking truth from facts are the ideological bases for good management of development zones. Over the past 30 years, development zones have adhered to mental emancipation, sought truth from facts, adjusted reforming measures according to local conditions, followed the objective laws of regional development, emphasized taking stock of real situations, given full play to the advantages of resources such as land, market and labor, accurately set the development orientation and actively explored the mode of development. ETDZs are mostly located in large cities where industries are concentrated. They have developed manufacturing industry, attracted foreign investment and facilitated exporting. HTDZs are mostly located in places where colleges and scientific research institutions cluster. They are devoted to industrializing new and high technologies. Border economic cooperation zones, located in border regions, actively develop processing trade with neighboring countries. Bonded zones are situated in port cities and are aimed at expanding export volume and developing the port cities.

Second, adherence to system reform and opening up has provided the decisive momentum for the rapid development of development zones. The zones were built and developed when China's economic system was being transformed. Their main purpose was to develop the economy. Development zones were required to adhere to reform and opening up so that they could remain alive and vigorous, gain impetus and constantly attain new achievements. Years of practice have testified that only if development zones boldly implement reform and are innovative in every aspect can they remain vigorous and push their causes forward. Development zones are characterized by an export-oriented economy and stand at the forefront of opening up to the outside world. They actively take over international industrial transfer and absorb foreign advanced technologies and management experience. Their openness is not only embodied through their ability to attract investment, but also through their management and investment environment. Practice has also proved that development zones will only keep on improving their levels of development if they continuously perfect their investment climate in compliance with international practice and persist in integrating comprehensively with international capital, market, services and concepts.

Third, by adhering to the correct development guideline and scientific development planning, we strongly guarantee the growth of development zones. From the outset, the Chinese government has set clear guidelines and objectives for the various national development zones. Different requirements have applied to different periods. Not long after their establishment, development zones have made the policy 'three focuses, one devotion', which involved focusing on utilizing foreign investment, industry and exports, and being devoted to developing high and new technological industry. According to the development practice, in 2004, the State Council proposed another policy called 'three focuses, two devotions and one promotion', which referred to focusing on raising the quality of foreign investment, on developing modern manufacturing industry and on optimizing export structure, devoted to developing high and new technology industries and to developing a high value-added service industry, and promoting the transformation of national ETDZs into multi-functional comprehensive industrial zones. The policy added a new layer of meaning to the old one. The strategic objectives for high and new technological zones are 'to develop high and new technologies, to open up high and new technological industries', and 'the quaternity' that was to be proposed later ('The quaternity' refers to trying to become an important carrier to promote technological advancement and to enhance the ability to innovate independently, to be a powerful engine that drives the adjustment of regional economic structure and the transformation of economic growth mode, to be a service platform behind new and high technological enterprises that compete globally, and to be battle hardened so that they can become part of the global elite in terms of new and high technological industry.)

Chapter 6

What are the Features of Representative Development Zones in China?

6.1 The construction and development of Shenzhen SEZ

Shenzhen SEZ was born in 1979 amid the tide of reform and opening up. This birth was a natural response to the needs of reform and opening up. In May 2010, the State Council approved the expansion of the zone to cover the whole city, a signal that Shenzhen had entered the era of turning into a large special zone. Over the past 30 years, Shenzhen SEZ has fully played its role as an 'experimental area', a 'window', 'pacesetter' and 'demonstration zone'. Its economy grew by an average of 25.8% annually, leaping to the forefront of China's large and medium-sized cities. Once a small and remote border town, Shenzhen has grown rapidly into a large, modernized and globalized city with sophisticated transportation, complete municipal functions, advanced facilities, a sound legal system and beautiful environment. Shenzhen has worked a miracle in the global history of industrialization, urbanization and modernization.

6.1.1 The process of developing and opening up Shenzhen SEZ

Prior to reform and opening up, what is now called Shenzhen SEZ kept its original name of Bao'an county. On August 26, 1980 Shenzhen SEZ was officially established. Since then, the zone has confronted the severe challenge of 'fighting with its back to the river' – life-or-death reform. Throughout the past 30 years, Shenzhen has adhered to the spirit of reform and opening up and fully played its part as a 'window' and 'experimental area'. The process of its reform and opening up falls into four separate periods.

The early period of reform and opening up (1980-1985) With a view to breaking the shackles of old systems during its early stage of reform, Shenzhen SEZ took market as the orientation of development and removing price control and reforming infrastructure construction system as the breakthrough points. It began to reform government institutions, the systems of salary, infrastructure construction, price, employment, cadre personnel, planning and management, and secured considerable achievements. Reform at this stage was characterized by the efforts to 'break the shell and carve out a trail' for construction and opening up.

Soon after the zone was built, the support granted by the central government to Shenzhen was confined to policy, not capital. In order to fix the problems that emerged during the large-scale construction of the city's infrastructure, Shenzhen municipal party committee and municipal government bravely reformed the system of infrastructure construction. First, by introducing the bidding and tendering system as a breakthrough, the government granted the zone's contractors a comparatively large degree of autonomy, which stimulated their enthusiasm and creativity. Up to 1985, tendered projects took up more than 90% of all infrastructure projects; more than 400 tendered projects had been completed and the construction area totaled 5m square meters. The results brought on by the reform were impressive.

Second, it reformed the price system. After the SEZ was set up, the number of migrant workers rose sharply, causing difficulties for planning and distribution and a shortage of agricultural and sideline products. This severely undermined the construction of the zone. In 1982, Shenzhen municipal government decided to reform the price system. The policy guiding price reform was 'mainly to regulate, combine regulation and control, and straighten out the price system step by step'. Control over the price of commodities except for grain, cooking oil and meat were lifted prior to 1984.

Third, it reformed the salary system. With the removal of the 'iron rice bowl' (a symbol of egalitarianism that ignored how much work was performed) as a way out, salary reform was comprehensively implemented in enterprises, government offices and public institutions, which greatly incentivized constructors. This reform in Shenzhen influenced national salary system reform.

And fourth, it reformed the employment system. Many foreign business people came to Shenzhen to invest and build factories, but the old employment system was at odds with the prevailing trend. The municipal party committee and government fearlessly broke the 'iron rice bowl' employment system in which people were all appointed by the government to certain working posts and adopted the 'two-way selection system' in which the employer selects the prospective employee and vice versa. No trace of assignment or appointment remained. The employment system was gradually marketized. The labor contract system was gradually applied to all employees in Shenzhen SEZ. This reform mostly satisfied the employment needs of the mixed ownership economy. Due to employment reform, corresponding labor markets emerged in response to prevailing conditions. During this period, economic system reform in Shenzhen was particularly tough because this was the first SEZ in China, a country long dominated by the planned economic system. Everything was like 'crossing the river by fumbling for stones as footholds'. Along with the reform emerged all kinds of blame and fault-finding. However, Shenzhen finally managed to carve a way out, laying a solid foundation for more supportive and comprehensive reforms of market-oriented economic systems to come. In January 1984, Deng Xiaoping made his first inspection of Shenzhen and publicly and fully endorsed the journey made by Shenzhen SEZ: "The development and experience of Shenzhen prove that our policy to build SEZs is correct."

The period of pushing forward reform and opening up on all fronts (1986-1992) To follow the requirements and directions of the central committee of the party and the State Council, Shenzhen SEZ entered a new period of exploring how to develop an export-oriented economy outside the planned economic system and how to comprehensively carry out market economic system reform.

The party committee of Shenzhen municipality proposed to upgrade SEZ reform by replacing partial reforms with comprehensive ones, and by supplanting individual reforms with systematic ones. The main measures to realize these reforms were as follows: first, the zone led the shareholding reform in SOEs by innovating the management system of state-owned assets, putting in place enterprise contract and shareholding systems and thus allowing the transfer of property rights and bankruptcy. Second, the zone reformed the financial system and built a multi-level, open financial market. It brought in a group of foreign banks and built regional joint-stock banks such as China Merchants Bank and Shenzhen Development Bank. The zone established the nation's first center for foreign exchange regulation, built a non-ferrous metal futures market, issued shares and built a securities exchange. Third, the zone reformed the land management system in which any use of state-owned land required a payment. It also sold land through public auction for the first time. Fourth, the zone boldly reformed government institutions and implemented the civil servant system. Fifth, it reformed the housing system, gradually converting houses into commodities for sale. Sixth, the zone deepened reform of the labor and salary system, practiced the labor contract system and built a social security system. Seventh, the zone encouraged and supported private scientific and technological enterprises to develop, and many private scientific and technological enterprises sprang up including Huawei and Zhongxing.

Through these supporting reforms, the shackles of the old systems were mostly broken; the economic system and operation mechanism that let market regulation play a key role and the regulation of planning work as a supplement were basically formed. In 1992, with the contribution of many parties, Shenzhen Municipal People's Congress and its standing committee together with Shenzhen people's government were granted the power to pass laws and regulations. With the legislative power of an SEZ, Shenzhen immediately made a number of well-planned laws and regulations that were well suited to the market economic system. These laws and regulations that met the requirements of the development of the zone strongly guaranteed the success of reform and opening up and ensured rapid economic construction in Shenzhen SEZ. More important, they provided fresh experience and set an example to the whole nation in terms of building a legal system to meet the requirements of the socialist market economy. In the spring of 1992, Deng Xiaoping inspected Shenzhen once more and reaffirmed that Shenzhen SEZ's achievements were associated with reform and opening up. He said: "The achievements of Shenzhen's construction have clearly told those people who have various concerns that the special zone is 'socialist' rather than 'capitalist'." He added: "One important nugget of Shenzhen's experience is boldness."

The period of deepening reform and opening up (1993-2002) Deng Xiaoping's 'southern tour speech' and the 14th National Congress of the CPC confirmed that our reform and opening up had entered a new period. In the past, Shenzhen SEZ mainly relied on preferential policies of the central government; in this period, it was concerned with improving its overall quality and creating innovative advantages. This period revolved around making general objectives for the socialist market economic system. Shenzhen continued to deepen its exploration into aspects such as establishing the modern corporate system, perfecting the market system, transforming government functions, perfecting the social security system, and building the law and a regulatory system suitable for a market economy. The exploration formed the basic framework for the socialist market economic system. The principal measures were: the zone deepened the reform of SOEs and built the modern corporate system; it further reformed the system of state-owned assets management and built a three-level supervision and operation system of state-owned assets management; it perfected the structure of ownership and promoted the private economy; it deepened reform of the commerce and trade system, innovated the financial services system, built a foreign exchange trade center and a property rights exchange market, develop the technological sector, cultivated the investment market, introduced Shenzhen Stock Exchange's small and medium-sized enterprises board and perfected the labor market; meanwhile, it made more efforts to transform government functions, greatly reduced the number of items subject to administrative examination and approval, endeavored to reform the financial system, reformed the government procurement system, and accelerated reform of the investment and finance system; it deepened reform of the distribution system and advocated an annual salary system for enterprise operators; correspondingly, in order to support the social security system, it reformed the medical, pension and work-related injury systems; it governed the city by law, reformed the administrative system and fully practiced the national civil servant system. By deepening reform, Shenzhen's economy surged, maintaining an annual growth rate of around 20%. Three pillars of the national economy were formed: new and high technology, modern logistics and modern finance. The gross value of production increased from Rmb100bn in 1996 to Rmb200bn in 1998 and Rmb300bn in 2002. Shenzhen climbed to become the nation's leading large or medium-sized city in terms of overall economic strength.

The comprehensive coordinated period of reform and opening up (2003-present) In 2003, Hu Jintao inspected Shenzhen and required the city to accelerate, guide and coordinate its development, and keep itself ahead of the pace of national development. In 2006, Shenzhen was the first city in China to propose making itself a national entrepreneurial city, promoting innovation as the leading strategy for its development. In 2008, it set the objective to construct itself into a national innovative city and a socialist demonstration city with Chinese characteristics. In December 2008, the State Council approved *Outline Plan for the Reform and Development of the Pearl River Delta*. From a national level, the outline clearly defined Shenzhen's important position as 'one district, four cities': trial district for comprehensive coordinated reform; national economic center city; national entrepreneurial city; socialist demonstration city with Chinese characteristics; and international city. Local financial revenue climbed by Rmb10bn for five years in succession, from Rmb41.238bn in 2005 to Rmb88.082bn in 2009. From 2003 to 2012, Shenzhen contributed a total of more than Rmb1tn of revenue to the central government. Today, Shenzhen is striving to establish itself as 'the trial district for comprehensive coordinated reform; national economic center city; national entrepreneurial city; socialist demonstration city with Chinese characteristics; and international city'. Shenzhen SEZ is planning its future modeled on a 'large special zone'. It will make fullest use of its legislative power, then turn its attention to the actual situation in Shenzhen region, publishing regional legislation to help make itself the first socialist city governed by law. Such legislation will help Shenzhen develop faster. As the 'test base' and 'window' of China's reform and opening up, Shenzhen takes seriously the concern and hope of Deng Xiaoping, the chief architect of reform and opening up, and will never forget the blood and sweat of the many reform predecessors and constructors. As an example of socialism with Chinese characteristics, as a pioneering district and demonstration city that shows to the world the vitality of socialism with Chinese characteristics, Shenzhen will keep its pioneering spirit, youth and vitality and create an even better future from a new start.

6.1.2 The historic achievements made by Shenzhen SEZ in terms of reform and opening up

The historic achievements made by Shenzhen SEZ over the past three decades can be ascribed to the following five reasons.

First, Shenzhen brought into full play its role as 'a testing field' in system reform. Since the day it was created, Shenzhen SEZ has borne in mind the central government's strategic significance in building the zone. Shenzhen was daring, had a pioneering spirit, and tried its best to blaze a new trail for reforming the old system and building the socialist market economy. Shenzhen combined the basic socialist economic system with the development of a market economy, the dominance of public ownership with the development of an economy with different types of ownership, the dominance of distribution according to work with distribution according to production factors, and reform of the economic base with reform of the superstructure. From individual reforms to comprehensive coordinated reform, from economic reforms to reforms in other fields, Shenzhen was the first to build a comparatively perfect socialist market economic system and a corresponding operation system. Shenzhen was the first to reform the infrastructure construction system and to practice the system of bidding and contracting. It was the first to reform the employment and salary systems and to practice the labor contract and floating wage systems. Shenzhen was the first to reform the planning management and price systems, to reduce mandatory plans and indexes in kind, and to lift price controls. Shenzhen was the first to reform the cadre deployment system and to recruit according to talent. It was the first to promote enterprise property rights, to allow the usufruct of state-owned land to be transferred with payment and to accelerate the commercialization and marketization of production factors. Shenzhen was the first to reform the housing system, unemployment insurance, endowment insurance and medical insurance, and to build a relatively perfect social security system. It was the first to introduce the shareholding system into SOEs and to constantly perfect the modern corporate system. Shenzhen's bold exploration and successful practice associated with the reform of the market economy emancipated and developed social productivity, and created the concept of the 'Shenzhen speed', which amazed the world. From 1979 to 2013, Shenzhen's gross production value increased by 30% annually.

Second, Shenzhen played the role of a 'window' in the opening up program. The establishment of Shenzhen SEZ was a great step in opening up to the outside, as well as a new test of using foreign capital, technologies and management experience to develop the socialist economy. Shenzhen SEZ had consistently adhered to the strategy of expanding opening up and developing an export-oriented economy. Shenzhen took advantage of its geographical proximity to Hong Kong and Macau, actively utilizing domestic and international resources, taking the lead in bringing about Sino-foreign joint ventures, Sino-foreign cooperation and wholly foreign-owned enterprises, actively absorbing and utilizing foreign investment, bringing in advanced technology and management experience, expanding exports, communicating and cooperating with the world, and gradually constructing an economic operation system that is suited to the development of an export-oriented economy. Shenzhen's exploration was beneficial to China as it decided on the pattern of opening up and implemented the strategy of developing an export-oriented economy in coastal regions. Shenzhen became an important window through which China opened up and engaged with the outside world. Shenzhen's import and export trade ranked first among China's large and medium-sized cities for 20 consecutive years. Today, businesses from more than 90 countries and districts have invested in Shenzhen, and the total foreign investment that Shenzhen has utilized is close to US$40bn. More than 150 of the world's top 500 enterprises have set up companies or plants in Shenzhen. Meanwhile, Shenzhen's enterprises are taking an active part in global economic activities and follow the strategy of 'going global'. A number of famous transnational enterprises have flourished.

Third, Shenzhen is a 'pacesetter' in self-dependent innovation. Innovation is the life and soul of the development of SEZs. While pro-actively reforming and innovating the economic system, Shenzhen SEZ enthusiastically promoted independent scientific and technological innovation, searched hard for a new way to incorporate science and technology in the economy, and tried to occupy the high ground of new and high technologies and their industrialization. Shenzhen has developed new economic, industrial and technological advantages and taken the lead in building a comparatively complete regional innovation system that is market-oriented. The innovation system takes industrialization as the key aim, enterprises as the participants, and integrates government resources, industries, universities, research institutions and investment. Shenzhen used to be a city dominated by trade, real estate and processing industry. By persistently strengthening innovation, Shenzhen has grown into a city with the highest value output and export levels of high and new technological products. Shenzhen has become an important national base for researching and developing high and new technologies, for transforming achievements and for exporting and processing products, as well as an important trade center. Since 1992, the output value of high and new technology products in Shenzhen has increased by more than 45% a year, and the annual increase in the number of patents applied has exceeded 30%. Today, independent intellectual property rights apply to 58% of all Shenzhen's new and high technological products. Shenzhen has the most patents for invention and the most applications for Patent Cooperation Treaty patents among China's large and medium-sized cities for several consecutive years. It is home to 80 of China's 'top brands' and three of the country's 'world top brands', ranking first among the country's large and medium-sized cities. A group of high-tech enterprises represented by Huawei, Zhongxing and Dazu Laser have sprung up; they are characterized by self-innovation and are competitive and influential across the world. Shenzhen has formed a high-level industrial structure with high and new technological industry as its pillar. With its excellent performance in developing high and new technological industry and in self-innovation, Shenzhen has become the first national pilot city in terms of independent innovation. Shenzhen is brave enough to be the pioneer of the nation's strategy to pursue independent innovation and has garnered experiences in accelerating structural adjustment, optimization and upgrading and in fundamentally transforming the economic growth mode.

Fourth, Shenzhen played the role of a 'demonstration area' to showcase socialist modernization with Chinese characteristics. After it was created, Shenzhen SEZ made great efforts to push forward socialist modernization. It quickly became a modernized metropolis with a prosperous economy, beautiful environment, complete political, economic, cultural and social functions, and a sound legal system. It created a miracle of industrialization, urbanization and modernization in world history and played an exemplary role in national socialist modernization. Meanwhile, Shenzhen persisted in serving the development of the whole nation. Drawing on its advantages of capital, technology, talent, information and management, Shenzhen tried its best to cooperate economically with neighboring regions and other provinces and cities, in order to facilitate regional resource integration, complement each other's advantages and drive economic development in other areas. Shenzhen took seriously the strategic thinking of 'two overall blueprints' and earnestly supported underdeveloped districts as required by the central and provincial governments. It supported 10 provinces (or districts) and around 60 counties (or cities), with a total contribution of more than Rmb8bn. Shenzhen contributed greatly to the coordination of regional development and to the realization of common wealth. It played an important radiation and guiding role in national socialist modernization.

Fifth, Shenzhen greatly facilitated the smooth return of Hong Kong and Macau to China and helped them to maintain prosperity and stability. 'One country, two systems' is a grand idea that was masterminded by Deng Xiaoping and has enabled national reunification. It is also an important element of socialist theory with Chinese characteristics. Geographically close to Hong Kong and Macau, Shenzhen serves as the node to implement 'one country, two systems'. The establishment and development of Shenzhen SEZ was of strategic significance for facilitating the smooth return of Hong Kong and Macau to mainland China and for helping maintain long-term prosperity and stability. Since reform and opening up, Shenzhen has adopted a flexible management system and pursued special preferential policies. It has attracted many people from Hong Kong and Macau to invest and conduct business. Projects with direct investment from Hong Kong account for 80% of all projects in Shenzhen involving investment from outside mainland China; the total value of investment sourced only from Hong Kong accounts for more than 60% of the total value of all foreign-sourced investments. Many Hong Kong and Macau enterprises have developed rapidly by drawing on Shenzhen's location, resources, cost advantage and abundant labor supply.

They have enjoyed the benefits brought about by reform and opening up and the policy of 'one country, two systems'. While their economic connections are getting ever closer, Shenzhen, Hong Kong and Macau are experiencing more communication and cooperation in the fields of transportation, science and technology, culture, education and travel. They have created a favorable situation in which they complement each other's advantages, promote one other and develop together. Their cooperative relations in all aspects have become even more intimate. In addition, since reform and opening up, Shenzhen's economy and society have developed continuously, rapidly and healthily. It is improving day by day. People's living standards have improved very fast. All these developments have made the people of Hong Kong and Macau feel more identified with the motherland and enabled them to love the motherland even more. And their confidence in reform and opening up and the policy of 'one country, two systems' has been greatly boosted.

6.1.3 The basic experience of Shenzhen SEZ in terms of reform and opening up

The practices and achievements of Shenzhen SEZ have fully proved that reform and opening up satisfies the party and the people, follows the prevailing trend, is a key choice that decides the fate of contemporary China and is the only road that leads to the construction and development of socialism with Chinese characteristics and to the rejuvenation of the nation. After many years of reform and opening up, Shenzhen SEZ has made glorious achievements that amaze the world and accumulated very precious experience that boils down to the following five points.

First, we must cling to taking the socialist theoretical system with Chinese characteristics as the guideline. The establishment and development of Shenzhen SEZ *per se* was the product of the party when it was innovating and practicing socialist theories with Chinese characteristics. Throughout the whole process, Shenzhen SEZ persisted in exploring and practicing under the guidance of Deng Xiaoping Theory, the important thought of the 'three represents' and the guiding principles from Comrade Xi Jinping's major speeches and 'scientific outlook on development'. During this time, politically, Shenzhen adhered to the 'four cardinal principles' and socialist orientation. Economically, it has adhered to the basic economic system that is dominated by public ownership and allows different kinds of ownership to flourish simultaneously. In terms of ideology and culture, it has adhered to the socialist core value system. In terms of social development, it has persisted in improving people's livelihoods and promoting social harmony. In terms of specific practices relating to reform and development, it has always followed the guidance of the socialist theoretical system with Chinese characteristics in all its practices, such as the reform of ownership, the reform of the land and price systems, the reform of the distribution system, the reform of the employment and personnel system, the reform of the management system, the reform of cultural and social management systems, and the handling of relations between efficiency and fairness, development and stability, planning and market, material civilization and spiritual civilization, democracy and legislation, economic system reform and administrative system reform, and urban construction and environmental protection. As a consequence, Shenzhen has achieved many successes, verifying and enriching the socialist theoretical system with Chinese characteristics. Shenzhen's practices have fully proved that the socialist theoretical system with Chinese characteristics is a powerful theological weapon that helps the SEZ operate in the right direction and to record further glorious achievements. Shenzhen's practices have also proved that the socialist theoretical system with Chinese characteristics is a scientific system that is capable of guiding reform and opening up as well as modernizing contemporary China.

The second point is that we must always adhere to mental emancipation. The most distinct feature of Shenzhen's reform and opening up is mental emancipation. Reform and opening up is the people's great new revolution led by the party in a new era. There is no ready-made theoretical model that offers guidance to China's reform in the Marxist classics; nor is there any real experience in history of the international communist movement to reference. So, we must keep on emancipating our minds, exploring and practicing. In retrospect, every great breakthrough or achievement made by Shenzhen while carrying out reform and opening up had its root in, and was enhanced by, mental emancipation. At the early stage of reform and opening up, Shenzhen SEZ adhered to mental emancipation, boldly making explorations based on reality, taking the lead in breaking ossified modes of thinking and practices, launching assaults one after another at the 'forbidden zones' of traditional concepts and initiating national reform and opening up. In the historical process of building and perfecting the socialist market economic system, Shenzhen SEZ continued to emancipate the mind, stuck to the criteria of 'three beneficials', continuously deepened the reform of the traditional planned economic system, focused on establishing and perfecting the socialist market economy, formed the basic framework of the socialist market economy and made explorations to establish and perfect the national socialist market economic system. After entering the new century and coming into the new stage of reform, Shenzhen SEZ has further emancipated the mind, deeply implemented the significant strategic thought of the party central committee such as the 'scientific outlook on development and the construction of a harmonious society', endeavored to change the traditional notion and mode of development, coordinated the development of the economy, politics, culture, society and ecology ('five in one'), and taken new steps to continue to practice and explore socialism with Chinese characteristics. Shenzhen's practice has testified to the fact that mental emancipation is the source of momentum for the take-off of the SEZs, a magic instrument for the development of socialism with Chinese characteristics, and a basic experience that we must always adhere to when we push forward reform and opening up and socialist modernization.

The third point is that we must adhere to reform oriented toward the socialist market economy. Since it was established, Shenzhen SEZ has insisted on starting from the national situation, following economic laws, boldly breaking the rigid planned economic system, and taking the lead in pushing forward the reform and innovation of the market economic system. Setting aside arguments such as 'capitalist or socialist' and 'public or private', Shenzhen has always adhered to the basic socialist economic system that is dominated by public ownership and allows different types of ownership to develop simultaneously and has taken the right direction. While steadfastly consolidating and developing the public economy, Shenzhen persisted in marketization, and was the first to encourage, support and guide the development of the non-public economy, protect all sectors of the economy regardless of ownership and let them compete on an equal basis and promote one another. Shenzhen was the first to introduce the shareholding system into SOEs, optimize the layout and structure of the state-owned economy, and strengthen the vitality, controlling force and influence of the state-owned economy. Shenzhen was the first to build a unified, open and modern market system with orderly competition, and actively develop the markets of all kinds of production factors. Shenzhen was the first to reform prices, labor, personnel, distribution, land, finance and tax, and banking. Through 'bringing in' and 'going out', Shenzhen was the first to expand the depth and breadth of opening up, improve the export-oriented economy, form new advantages in international economic cooperation and competition against the background of economic globalization, transform the growth pattern of foreign trade, accelerate the transformation and upgrade of processing trade, innovate the way of utilizing foreign investment, optimize the structure of foreign capital utilization, and guarantee the continuous, healthy and stable development of the economy. Shenzhen's experience has proved that the transition from highly centralized planned economy to vigorous socialist market economy is a sure choice of reform and opening up, as well as the right path for China's national situation and one that follows objective laws.

The fourth point is that we must dare to absorb and learn from all the excellent achievements of human civilization. As a window of reform and opening up, since its establishment, Shenzhen SEZ has boldly introduced foreign capital, technology, information, talent and management, and meanwhile selectively absorbed and learnt from the successful experience and systems of different countries around the world. Through digestion, absorption and re-innovation, Shenzhen was the first to come up with an economic operation system that met the requirements of the socialist market economy and was suitable to China's national situation and international accepted practice. In the process of reform and opening up, Shenzhen proposed to 'reject the bad but not the foreign', insisted on the dominance of the socialist culture, inherited the good traditions of the national culture, actively assimilated the excellent civilization of other countries and regions, and formed a vigorous culture that is specific to Shenzhen SEZ, has Chinese characteristics, honors innovation, tolerates failure, praises realism and pursues excellence. Shenzhen's China Hi-tech Fair and China International Cultural Industry Fair not only provide important platforms from where Chinese scientific and technological products and cultural and artistic works can go out to the world, but also offer a way for people to bring in and learn from foreign advanced science and technology and culture. In recent years, Shenzhen has set an ambitious objective to build itself into an international city and learn from and catch up with advanced global cities. This is a significant strategic measure adopted by Shenzhen in order to further the depth and breadth of its opening up, and participate in international cooperation and competition across a wider range, in more fields and at higher levels, against the background of economic globalization. Shenzhen's experience has fully proved that reform and opening up demands a mind that is as open and tolerant as an ocean, taking water from hundreds of rivers, and that only if we boldly absorb and learn from all the achievements of human civilization can we better develop socialism with Chinese characteristics.

And the fifth point is that we must persist in pushing forward the development of science and promoting social harmony. Shenzhen started the reform and opening up much earlier than other cities in China, so its economic strength quickly surged to the forefront among large and medium-sized cities. However, it also encountered tension between development and the natural system and the contradiction between development and the social system earlier than other cities. Its development was obviously limited by space, resources, population and environment, and was severely challenged in terms of public security, urban management, population management and social undertakings. In recent years, Shenzhen has seriously implemented the significant strategic ideas of the party central committee such as the 'scientific outlook on development' and the 'construction of a harmonious society'; proposed the strategic objective of 'building a harmonious and efficient Shenzhen', and sought to reform the developmental mode. Shenzhen has been integrating economic growth speed, quality and efficiency, laying emphasis on the improvement of quality and efficiency; it has been integrating the expansion of economic scale with the optimization of economic structure, putting emphasis on the latter; it has also been integrating the promotion of economic growth with the improvement of development capability, putting emphasis on the latter; it has been integrating short-term and long-term interests, with an emphasis on social and economic sustainable development. With its economy expanding rapidly, its society being peaceful, harmonious and stable, and its ecological environment improving, Shenzhen symbolizes a benign development tendency. Its practices have fully proved that, in order to adapt to the new situation and new tasks, to continue reform and opening up, and to keep on exploring and innovating the developmental mode, we shall inevitably choose to adhere to scientific development and promote social harmony.

Deng Xiaoping's inspection tour of Guangdong in 1992 (Photograph by Niu Zhengwu, released by Xinhua News Agency)

6.2 The construction and development of Pudong New District

6.2.1 The development, opening up and achievements of Pudong New District

(1) **The development and opening up of Pudong New District** On a visit to Shanghai on February 18, 1990, Deng Xiaoping said that the development of Pudong was a crucial step that will have a far-reaching impact on the restoration of Shanghai's vitality and on the development of the Yangtze River basin and even the whole nation. On April 18, 1990, the State Council officially approved Shanghai's proposals on how to accelerate the development of Pudong and agreed to allow Pudong to enjoy the same policies as ETDZs, as well as some of the policies afforded to SEZs. On May 3, 1990, the Pudong Development Office under the People's Government of Shanghai Municipality was founded. In April 1991, the development of Pudong was formally listed as a national development strategy.

(2) **The major periods of Pudong New District's development and opening up** The first period covered the early years from 1990 to 1995. The tasks in this period included making plans, renovating the environment, actively creating conditions to attract foreign investment, and building bonded zones, export processing zones, high science and technology parks, finance and trade zones in different areas, step by step. During this period, Pudong finished the first round of 10 infrastructure construction projects mainly relating to transportation, communication and energy. The basic objective in this period was to take advantage of the policies granted to Pudong by the central government that allowed Pudong to reform and open up way ahead of other districts on a trial basis. These policies effectively boosted the combination of financial support with an innovative financing mechanism, combining a growing utilization of foreign capital with expanding market access, and devolution of authority with system innovation.

The second period covered 1996 to 2000. In this period, relatively complete supportive infrastructure was preliminarily built. Some Rmb100bn of investment was put into the second round of infrastructure construction projects that focused on airports, national information infrastructure and deepwater ports. The development of Lujiazui Finance and Trade Zone and Waigaoqiao Bonded Zone, along with their finance and trading functions, was accelerated. The central status of production factors in market distribution was demonstrated for the first time. The three major functions of Waigaoqiao Bonded Zone – international trade, processing trade and modern logistics –

were full developed. The functions of the high-tech industry area concerning technological innovation and industrialization were strengthened, too. The industrial structure was fully upgraded, and a new industrial system framework centered on financial trade and high-tech was formed.

The third period spanned 2001 to 2010 when the zone's functions were developed rapidly. In this period, Pudong New District took four national development zones as the carriers, developed its functions more deeply, constantly improved its comprehensive functions, gradually perfected its market mechanism, kept on optimizing its economic operation environment, and diverted its economic growth point to the development of the headquarters economy and R&D economy. Its economy developed rapidly. In 2005, the State Council officially approved Pudong New District to carry out pilot comprehensive coordinated reform, which marked that the reform had entered a new period and that the development of Pudong had entered a new stage, aimed at building Pudong into an export-oriented modern urban area with multiple functions.

After more than 20 years of construction and development, Pudong New District has become a densely populated area with high levels of planning and operation. Its population density reached 3,293 per square kilometer. Its GDP per capita has exceeded US$18,700. A new industrial system dominated by new and high technologies and modern service industry has already taken shape. This can be illustrated in the following aspects.

First, Pudong's comprehensive coordinated economic strength grew quickly. The contribution made by Pudong New District to Shanghai's overall economic growth increased every year. Pudong has become an important growth point in the development of Shanghai's economy. Accounting for just one fifth of Shanghai's population and one sixth of its area, Pudong generated almost a quarter of Shanghai's GDP and gross industrial output value and a half of its foreign trade value, and attracted a third of Shanghai's foreign direct investment. Pudong's gross output value increased from Rmb6.024bn in 1990 to Rmb600bn in 2012, with the value-added index rising from 100 to 1,000 over the same period. Pudong accounted for 7.96% of Shanghai's gross output value in 1990, rising to 32% in 2012. The economic status of Pudong in the municipality was increasing day by day. In 2012, its total financial revenue was Rmb236.081bn, and local financial revenue increased to Rmb55bn from Rmb0.6bn, a 92-fold increase. With the industrial structure being adjusted for more than 20 years, the ratio of the primary, secondary and tertiary sectors in terms of the number of companies in each sector was transformed, from 3.7 : 76.2 : 20.1 to 0.5 : 39.2 : 60.3. The proportion of primary and secondary sectors decreased while the tertiary sector, which includes finance, insurance, modern logistics and information services, grew rapidly. However, in terms of output value, the tertiary sector was still slightly lower than that of the secondary sector.

Second, urban construction changed the face of the district in varying degrees on a daily basis. Between 1990 and 2012, the total investment in Pudong's fixed assets was more than Rmb2.2tn; the total length of roads built during the period was 11,961km. Pudong quickened the construction of important physical infrastructure, and completed a host of significant construction projects, such as Pudong international airport, Waigaoqiao port area and Shanghai Information Port, as well as municipal infrastructure including cross-river transportation, rail transportation and expressways. The process of urbanization continued its rapid momentum. The ecological environment improved. The urbanized area, either established or under construction, totaled 270 square kilometers. Pudong New District is now honored as a 'national environmental protection model district', 'national civilized district', 'national garden district', 'national sanitary district' and 'national advanced barrier-free construction district'. As China's only airport with two runways, Pudong international airport has become a tourist attraction in itself. The central green land of 100,000 square meters adds luster to Lujiazui Finance and Trade Zone.

Third, foreign business and inland-related enterprises strongly desire to invest in Pudong. Since 1990 when the planning began for Pudong to get off the ground, foreign investment has flooded into the area. In 2012, contractual foreign investment stood at US$7.286bn, increasing by 10.4% over the previous year, to reach a record high; the number of foreign-invested enterprises exceeded 20,000; the number of foreign investment programs exceeded 20,000. No fewer than 308 of the world's top 500 enterprises had companies or plants based in Pudong and they invested in more than 1,023 programs. There were 193 regional headquarters of transnational companies authorized and acknowledged by the Shanghai government, of which 59 were Asia-Pacific headquarters. The tertiary industry accounted for as much as 90% of foreign-invested programs. They mainly focused on modern service industries, such as commerce and trade, management of investment and assets, financial loans, logistics and professional consultancy.

Fourth, the developmental functions went ever deeper. Relying on four national development zones, Pudong deepened its functional development and built six functional areas. Lujiazui Finance and Trade Zone had more than 737 domestic and foreign financial institutions based there, including the Shanghai headquarters of People's Bank of China, 64 regional headquarters of transnational enterprises, 34 headquarters of large Chinese enterprises and more than 4,000 professional intermediary service agencies. Factor markets such as securities and property rights became more capable of gathering, radiating and distributing. Linkages between Waigaoqiao Bonded Zone and Waigaoqiao Port Area were built. The zones' functions in terms of export processing, international trade and bonded logistics were developed constantly. Their functions as harbors, airports and hubs were gradually strengthened, and they became important ports and hubs for logistics in the Yangtze River Delta and even across the whole nation. As for Jinqiao Export Processing Zone, its level of advanced manufacturing, futures and the property rights industry were improved and its research and development services were enhanced; its total investment, both domestic- and foreign-sourced, was worth US$11bn; more than 90 of its projects involved an investment of more than US$10m.

Fifth, enterprises were more capable of technological innovation. Pudong has built 10 national industrial bases, such as the national microelectronics industrial base, the national software export base and the national LED industrial base. A group of corporate R&D centers and innovative institutions such as scientific research institutions settled down in Pudong. In 2012, Pudong New District was awarded several national prizes for making advancements in science and technology, which directly reflected the innovation inherent in Pudong's enterprises. First, the enterprises made breakthroughs in fields with great potential for industrialization, and were at the high end of the industrial technology chain. Second, the enterprises made breakthroughs in fields that relate to the welfare of the nation and the public. Third, the enterprises were the main participants in producing, learning and researching. All these indicate that the enterprises in the new district are becoming more capable of self-innovation, signaling that Pudong's system of scientific and technological innovation with enterprises as the main participants has improved step by step.

Sixth, new breakthroughs were made in system innovation. Through persistent practice, Pudong New District creatively proposed a series of clear development thoughts, for example giving priority to financial trade, infrastructure and new and high technological industry, linking the east and west of Shanghai and coordinating their development, unifying urban and rural areas and developing them simultaneously, and emphasizing laws, rules, planning and talent. The reform and functional transformation of government institutions promoted the new management mode known as 'small government, big society'. 'Small government' means that the authorized size of administrative committees must be small; 'big society' calls for perfecting social service institutions according to the requirements of social development. The management mode of 'small government, big society' has played a positive role in promoting the transformation of government functions and nurturing the operation mechanism of the market economy.

6.2.2 The basic experience of Pudong New District in terms of development and opening up

First, the core experience within Pudong's development and opening up is to adhere to 'mental emancipation, trying and trialing first, reform and innovation'. While developing and carrying out the policy of opening up, Pudong New District always adheres to mental emancipation, observes the law of development, overcomes development bottlenecks, insists on taking transformation of the development mode as the main line, playing a pioneering role in reform and opening up, and constantly improving productivity. Pudong actively pushes the line of a controlling government becoming service-oriented, deepens reform of the administrative examination and approval system, creates an open, fair and impartial legal environment, and provides efficient and quality government services for the development of enterprises and the attraction of talented workers.

Second, the central measure of Pudong's development and opening up is to adhere to scientific development and the strategy of sustainable development. As far as attracting investment is concerned, Pudong is concerned with not just quantity, but quality as well; it pays more attention to improving the quality of foreign investment, optimizing industrial structure and expanding new functions. In terms of attracting investment, instead of focusing on the scale of projects as it used to do, Pudong puts more emphasis on using investment resources wisely and intensively, on cultivating a circular economy and on materializing sustainable development. Instead of stressing preferential policies with regard to attracting investment, Pudong puts more emphasis on giving play to the advantage of an integrated environment, and on enhancing the utilization of foreign investment. As far as developing a headquarters' economy is concerned, instead of being concerned with the transformation of single functions such as new buildings, Pudong is more concerned with the developing comprehensive functions such as landscape design, the provision of green space and efficient property services. As far as industrial development is concerned, instead of emphasizing the introduction of technologies and industrial agglomeration, Pudong puts more stress on self-innovation and the introduction of high and new technological industries so that its international competitiveness can be enhanced.

Third, adherence to 'making Shanghai prosperous, serving the whole nation and facing the world' is Pudong's path to the success of reform and opening up. In terms of economic globalization, Pudong New District has discovered the orientation of development, grasped the development opportunities, made great efforts to promote industrial upgrading and functional promotion through continuously expanding opening up, and attracted various resources such as technology, capital and intelligence from around the world. Pudong New District has built many important infrastructure facilities such as Pudong international airport, Yangshan deepwater port and Waigaoqiao port area, providing efficient and convenient platforms that connect international and domestic markets and enable Pudong to use international and domestic resources. Pudong keeps on expanding the scope of opening up, endeavors to take a broad and open outlook and accomplish comprehensive development. Pudong has expanded opening up from the manufacturing sector to international finance and insurance, international trade, international shipping, modern logistics, and so on. Its function of demonstration and radiation has been enhanced. Pudong's development and opening up is having an increasingly important impact on Shanghai and the wider region. It has become a powerful engine for Shanghai to reshape its political, cultural and social functions and to develop its economy rapidly. It has become a pioneer for the development of an open economy along the Yangtze River Delta and in the riparian region. It has become a key link for our nation to deepen reform and opening up from points to areas and to connect the past and the future.

Fourth, the central objective of Pudong's reform and opening up is to adhere to the value 'putting people first'. Pudong sticks to the development strategy of giving priority to employment and has created more jobs in the process of industrial upgrading and urban development. It has created more than a million new jobs and guaranteed the supply of human resources for foreign-invested enterprises. Pudong endeavors to change the urban-rural structure, makes efforts to promote modernized living areas and facilities, and the construction of an ecological environment, continuously enriches the urban living function, and tries to build an ecological urban area that is suitable for habitation and conducting business. Pudong was awarded the China Habitat Award, the United Nations Habitat Award and was named 'national garden-like urban area', 'national model urban area for environmental protection' and 'national civilized urban area'.

6.3 The construction and development of Suzhou Industrial Park

6.3.1 The major periods of the development and construction of Suzhou Industrial Park

Suzhou Industrial Park, approved by the State Council to be set up in February 1994, was a significant cooperative project between the Chinese and Singaporean governments. In terms of administrative division, Suzhou Industrial Park covers 288 square kilometers (the China-Singapore cooperative area covers 80 square kilometers), has a registered population of 352,000 and a resident population of 695,000. The developmental objective of the park is to become a high-tech industrial park that is internationally competitive and a globalized, modernized, informationized, ecological, creative and pleasant urban district. As a significant cooperative project between China and Singapore, Suzhou Industrial Park has always received high-level attention from the two governments. A China-Singapore joint steering council was formed, involving China's vice-premier and Singapore's deputy prime minister as chairmen. The two countries made clear that 'whatever conforms to the direction of reform can be tried first in the park, and what has no definite direction yet can also be tried in the park', which has helped create a development environment that allows an approach of 'go and try first'.

Since 1994, drawing on the successful experiences of other advanced districts at home and abroad, Suzhou Industrial Park has actively searched for the developmental road toward new industrialization and urban modernization that is well suited to the local circumstances. Its annual growth rate estimated by various economic indicators has been more than 30%. Its comprehensive development index ranks second among national development zones. It has created a development performance known as the 'four more than 100 billions' (its total tax revenue paid to the central government is more than Rmb165bn; its utilized foreign investment is valued at US$18.9bn; its total registered capital is Rmb197.2bn; and its output of new industries in 2010 was valued at Rmb147.2bn, accounting for 45.4% of the industrial enterprises above a designated scale, ranking first in the city). Accounting for 3.4% of Suzhou's land and 5.2% of its population, the park has created about 15% of Suzhou's economic output and become an important growth pole of economic and social development.

The construction of Suzhou Industrial Park can be divided into the following three periods.

The initial period (1992-1994) In the spring of 1992, Comrade Deng Xiaoping said in his 'southern tour speech': "The social order of Singapore is good. They run a tight ship. We should learn from their experience and do even better than them." This remark evoked a positive reaction from the leaders in Singapore. In September 1992, Senior Minister Lee Kuan Yew visited China with a delegation and expressed the wish to build, in cooperation with China, a vehicle from which China could learn from Singapore's experience. After that, China and Singapore began to negotiate over this project and made several cooperative field trips. Finally, they chose Suzhou in Jiangsu province as the right place for such a park. In February 1994, the State Council approved Suzhou to cooperate with Singapore and build a park with a planned area of 70 square kilometers. On February 26, 1994 in Beijing, the Chinese and Singaporean governments officially signed *The Agreement on Cooperatively Developing and Constructing Suzhou Industrial Park*. Suzhou municipal people's government, Jurong Town Corporation of Singapore and the consortium that invested in Singapore-Suzhou Industrial Park signed *The Agreement on Learning From and Using Singapore's Experience in Economic and Public Management* and *The General Business Agreement on Cooperatively Developing Suzhou Industrial Park*. In order to ensure the smooth implementation of the park programs, China and Singapore created the China-Singapore Joint Steering Council with China's vice-premier and Singapore's deputy prime minister as chairmen, and a bilateral working committee co-presided by Suzhou's mayor and chairman of Jurong Town Corporation. Singapore's Software Program Office under the Ministry of Trade and Industry and the park's Learning Singaporean Experience Office took charge of daily communication. With the permission of the former Ministry of Trade and Economic Cooperation, China-Singapore Suzhou Industrial Park Development Group (CSSD) was founded as the major participant in the development of the park. The first group of 14 foreign-invested projects including Samsung and the US-based BD settled in the park.

The foundation-laying period (1995-2000) During this period, drawing on Singapore's experience in urban planning and management, with the approval of Jiangsu provincial people's government, Suzhou and Singapore together made general and specific plans for the development of the park, started to construct important infrastructure and large-scale energy plants that supplied water, electricity, gas and other services, finished the initial construction of an area of 12 square kilometers, and filled the area with buildings and companies. Following the principle of 'simplicity, unification and high efficiency', the major participants of the park's administrative management – the Park Working Committee and the Park Management Committee – and other management systems were set up, and the professional business-attraction team and network were initially built. On June 28, 1999, the Chinese and Singaporean working teams signed the *Memorandum of Understanding about the Development of Suzhou Industrial Park*, raising the share proportion held by the Chinese consortium from 35% to 65%, letting China assume the responsibilities of the majority shareholder and taking charge of the major management work in the park.

The faster development period (2001-present) In 2001, after the adjustment of the China-Singapore share proportions, the park also adjusted its development objective and strategy as the new period required. From 'sparing no effort to head development toward the east' to the implementation of 'the three big plans – upgrading manufacturing, advancing science and technology, and doubling the service industry', and then to proposing a new 10-year development objective and the 'four demonstration zones' objective, with a higher starting point, higher standard and greater strength, the park has been constantly accelerating its development, has mostly finished infrastructure construction inside the China-Singapore cooperative zone and has constructed a road network and supporting facilities in neighboring towns. The park has built the Science and Technology Culture and Arts Center, the International Expo Center, the Administration and Services Center and many modernized supporting facilities relating to education, sanitation, commercial recreation and community services. The park insists on developing advanced manufacturing and modern service industries simultaneously, and keeps on increasing its efforts to attract business, investment and talent.

6.3.2 The major practices and features of the development and construction of Suzhou Industrial Park

After almost 20 years of development, Suzhou Industrial Park has become a flagship program for cooperation between China and Singapore, a pilot of reform and opening up, an international cooperation demonstration zone, and one of China's development zones that has been the fastest growing and most internationally competitive. Six factors have contributed greatly to this advantageous position.

First, senior leadership facilitated China-Singapore cooperation. In order to meet the necessary high standards, become highly efficient, provide quality services and ensure that Suzhou Industrial Park develops fully and smoothly, China and Singapore have established high-level leading work institutions that cover many aspects. The first aspect refers to the China-Singapore Joint Steering Council, which takes charge of big problems emerging in the course of developing and constructing Suzhou Industrial Park and learning from the experience of Singapore. China's vice-premier and Singapore's deputy prime minister are chairmen of the council, and members of the council include China's National Development and Reform Commission, Ministry of Science and Technology, Ministry of Commerce, Ministry of Finance, Ministry of Foreign Affairs, Ministry of Housing and Urban-Rural Development, Ministry of Land and Resources, General Administration of Customs, State Administration of Taxation, State Administration for Quality Supervision and Inspection and Quarantine, Jiangsu provincial people's government and Suzhou municipal people's government, and Singapore's Ministry of Trade and Industry, Ministry of Foreign Affairs, prime minister's office, Ministry of National Development and Ministry of Education. The second aspect refers to the China-Singapore Bilateral Working Committee co-presided by Suzhou's mayor and the chairman of Jurong Town Corporation; its members include Suzhou municipal people's government, Park Management Committee, and Singapore's Ministry of Trade and Industry together with its directors. The third aspect refers to the park's Learning from the Singaporean Experience Office and Singapore's Software Program Office of the Ministry of Trade and Industry taking charge of daily communication.

Second, we look to the future with scientific planning. 'Planning goes first' and 'planning is law' are key factors contributing to the park's success, and are among the park's development concepts that are most worthy of being promulgated. According to the overall objective of regional development, drawing on the advanced development experience of cities across the world, experts from China and Singapore made forward-looking regional plans, formulated and perfected the plans for more than 400 professional programs, scientifically designed urban functions associated with industry, commerce, trade, living and transportation, established the scientific development procedure – 'planning ahead of construction, from underground to ground' – and formed a rigorous and perfect planning system and a planning management system that followed the rules 'enforcing the laws strictly' and 'acting appropriately beforehand'. In terms of infrastructure construction, the park has learned from Singapore's practice of 'building infrastructure before the need emerges', follows the development concepts of 'enforcing laws strictly' and 'acting appropriately beforehand', and adopts the standard of 'nine connections and one smoothness'. In addition, the park not only strives to develop a modern service industry incorporating restaurants, hotels, finance, commerce, business and so on as social needs demand, but also actively builds public service facilities such as schools, science and technology museums, stadiums, neighborhood centers and community work stations, with a view to constantly enhancing regional social service functions.

Third, we practice the principle of developing creatively and managing efficiently. CSSD is a vehicle of cooperation between China and Singapore and the major participant in the early development of Suzhou Industrial Park. It is invested by consortiums from both countries; the Chinese consortium includes 14 large enterprise groups such as COFCO, COSCO, Sinochem and Huaneng; the Singaporean consortium consists of 24 shareholders comprising corporations controlled by the Singaporean government, powerful private corporations and famous transnational corporations. The management committee manages the park and is made up of 15 offices with different functions. By instilling the idea of 'pro-business and pro-people', enhancing the function of a one-stop service and implementing a social service commitment system, the committee has preliminarily formed a simple, unified and efficient service-oriented government, an 'all-process, all-dimension and all-day' service system, an open, impartial and fair market order, and a scientific, standard and transparent legal environment.

Fourth, we adhere to the transforming development mode and upgrading industries. The park has transformed the development mode, upgraded manufacturing industry, doubled the size of the service industry, advanced science and technology, optimized the ecology, doubled the nanotechnology industry, and doubled the finance industry in three years, carried out the 'Jinji Lake double-hundred talents' plan that was designed to cultivate and recruit innovative entrepreneurs, and implemented 'the eight grand plans' for boosting culture. The efforts to transform and upgrade have paid off. New industries have expanded rapidly. The park has spared no effort in developing strategic new industries that are led by nanotechnology and supported by five new industries including nanometer photoelectric new energy, biomedicine, converged communication, software and cartoon games, and environmental protection. In 2010, these new industries generated Rmb147.2bn-worth of output, taking up 45.4% of all industrial enterprises above a certain size, ranking first in the city. Nanotechnology and its related company brands have come to the fore. The scale of the park's three big industries, new-type flat-panel displays, energy conservation and environmental protection, and biomedicine, all account for more than one third of Suzhou's total in these industries. The park was granted titles by Jiangsu provincial government such as 'demonstration zone for the integration of information technology and industrialization', 'innovative science and technology park', 'energy conservation and environmental protection science and technology industrial park', 'biomedicine technology industrial park', and 'converged communication science and technology industrial park'.

Fifth, we strive to go global and innovate methods to attract business. The park always attaches the greatest importance to attracting investors. It actively works out ways to attract investors, builds pro-business networks and innovates appropriate methods. The park advances and advocates the concept of 'selecting business and investment', and favors capital-intensive, technology-intensive and flagship projects that conform with international training and certification standards. It targets Fortune 500 companies and projects related to them, brings in leading projects that are at the core of their relevant industries, and gets supportive projects to come in. Up to the end of 2010, Suzhou Industrial Park had introduced more than 4,000 foreign enterprises and US$40.3bn of contractual foreign investment; it utilized US$18.9bn of foreign investment. Of these, 137 projects involved Fortune 500 companies; 112 projects involved more than US$100m of investment, and seven projects had an investment of more than US$1bn. The park has ranked first among China's development zones for several consecutive years in terms of utilized foreign investment. In fields such as integrated circuits, LCDs, automobile and aviation components, software and service outsourcing, biomedicine and new nanometer materials and new energy, the park has formed industrial and competitive clusters. Occupying one hundred-thousandth of China's land, the park has created 3% of the nation's foreign trade, 3% of its IT output value, 15% of its integrated circuit output and 5% of offshore outsourcing output. A modern industrial system led by the high- and new-tech sector has already taken rough shape and has been supported by advanced manufacturing and modern tertiary industries. The park has become a powerful engine and a major growth pole to drive regional development.

Sixth, we keep on drawing talent and combining production and research. Following the guideline 'attracting people with policies, retaining people with careers, nurturing people with the environment', the park has adopted a new marketized human resource distribution system that conforms to international conventions, formed a market system that allows talent to migrate freely and an assessment system that classifies the talents required, and built a large information bank of top talent. At present, there are more than 400 scientific and technological enterprises and more than 20,000 senior professional and skilled workers of all kinds. The park has actively founded a professional education system to offer vocational and technical training. Eight colleges and nearly 10 training institutions have settled in. In the park, there are about 25,000 students, 600 of whom are doctoral students and 3,700 are postgraduates.

6.4 The practice and exploration of Kunshan ETDZ

6.4.1 The basic situation and development of Kunshan ETDZ

Kunshan is located in the east of the Yangtze River Delta, 45km to the west of downtown Shanghai and 22km to the east of downtown Suzhou. It sits as the eastern gate of Jiangsu province. Kunshan has an area of 921 square kilometers and a population of 1,647,000, of whom 730,000 are registered residents. Administratively, it has 10 towns under its jurisdiction. It also has a national ETDZ and three provincial development zones. Up to the end of 2012, more than 5,000 projects invested by 65 countries and regions had been authorized across the city. Among these projects, 63 were invested by transnational corporations that are listed among the Fortune 500; more than 3,800 enterprises invested by Taiwanese businessmen had been founded with a total investment of more than US$15bn, making Kunshan one of the places in mainland China with the highest density of Taiwanese investment. Kunshan ranks first among the top 100 counties (or county-level cities) in China in terms of comprehensive economic development. Importantly, its pillar industries, such as electronic information and precision machinery, have already formed a complete industrial chain. Kunshan is also home to the largest manufacturing base of laptops in the world: one out of every two laptops in the world is made in Kunshan.

On August 22, 1992, with approval from the State Council, Kunshan ETDZ was officially upgraded to a state-level ETDZ. Over the past 20 years, the overall economic strength of Kunshan ETDZ has made a historic leap forward, from 'relying on traditional industries to build the zone' through to 'using service industries to strengthen the zone'; from 'being driven by exports' to 'emphasizing both exports and domestic consumption'; from pushing forward 'industrialization' and 'urbanization' to constructing a comprehensive zone that 'integrates urban and industrial development'. Kunshan has introduced close to 2,000 projects involving investors from 45 countries and regions, including from Europe, the US, Japan, South Korea, Hong Kong, Macau and Taiwan. With Taiwanese businessmen contributing nearly 50% of all investment, Kunshan is the most famous destination of Taiwanese investment in mainland China. Kunshan has one of the highest densities of enterprises in China and the best capital output ratio. Kunshan has become a global IT manufacturing base. In 2011, Kunshan ETDZ's GDP was Rmb136.8bn; its total industrial output was Rmb515bn; its total value of foreign trade was US$69.7bn and its financial revenue was Rmb19.4bn, 248, 244, 398 and 325 times those in 1992 respectively, giving an average annual growth rate of more than 30%.

The 1980s: transformation from agriculture to industry In January 1983, Document No. 1 issued by the central government gave support to developing commune-level and production brigade enterprises. Kunshan did its utmost to promote horizontal economic cooperation, and accelerated the growth of township industries. Cashing in on the opportunities created by the national strategy to develop and open up coastal regions, Kunshan set up a new industrial zone in the southeast of the county at its own expense in August 1984, with a plan to 'draw on the advantages of Shanghai in the east, depending on third-tier cities in the west, developing ties with township enterprises, aiming at the nation, and trying to go global', thus enabling the historical leap forward from traditional agriculture to industry.

The 1990s: moving from internal to external In April 1990, the party central committee and the State Council made the strategic decision to develop Pudong. Immediately, Kunshan capitalized on this historic opportunity and made great efforts to pursue the strategy of using opening up to generate economic growth. After eight years of hard work, in August 1992, Kunshan ETDZ was formally approved by the State Council and began to lead the opening up of township industrial zones across the city. Thus, from developing township industries to developing an open economy, the transformation from 'internal to external' was successfully realized.

The 21st century: proceeding from low to high In terms of developmental mode, Kunshan is shifting from depending on land resources to expand outwardly, to depending on scientific and technological advancement to improve inwardly. Enterprises that were formerly scattered have become more clustered and are cooperating more. In terms of industrial structure, Kunshan is changing from being driven mainly by manufacturing to developing through both manufacturing and service industries. In terms of product mix, Kunshan's products are changing from being extensive and of low quality to being high quality. Kunshan's overall developmental level shows a new tendency to move up 'from low to high'. Kunshan's comprehensive economic strength ranks first among all the nation's counties or county-level cities. In recent years, against the background of the international financial crisis, Kunshan has taken the lead in working out a series of policies and measures to transform its developmental mode and to support the growth of a modern service industry, which, in turn, has quickly led to the rapid emergence of modern service sectors, such as outsourcing and logistics. At present, four large industrial clusters are taking shape in Huaqiao International Business Park, including service outsourcing, headquarters economy, logistics and business services. The park has become Jiangsu's only provincial-level development zone dominated by modern service industry and which is included in the first group of provincial service-outsourcing demonstration zones.

6.4.2 The practice and experience of Kunshan ETDZ

Over the last 20 years, Kunshan ETDZ has accumulated three 'heirlooms': first, the government is active in providing efficient services; second, drawing investment with industrial chains and perfecting the industrial support environment; and third, persistence in promoting self-innovation while opening itself up to the outside world.

Let us discuss each of these 'heirlooms' in detail.

1) Governmental push and efficient services As China's only national ETDZ to start from scratch and funded at its own expense, Kunshan ETDZ has the spirit of 'daring to strive for No.1', and has achieved some 'national firsts'. For example, Kunshan had the nation's first export processing zone and its first county-level overseas students venture park. With many firsts, 'Kunshan practice' has spread and has become a national treasure of all development zones.

In August 1984, Kunshan county party committee and government became the first in the nation to plan, raise money and build at its own expense China's first new industrial district, covering an area of 3.75 square kilometers. (The sources of money are known as the 'four somes': some borrowed from government, some borrowed from banks, some collected from the people as development fees and some contributed by public service institutions.) Through great efforts year after year, adhering to self-dependence and working hard, Kunshan has become stronger and carved out a path from nothing that keeps on extending further. Finally, in August 1992, the State Council recognized it as Kunshan ETDZ, the nation's first state-approved development zone located in a county (city). During the process, one of the guarantees for success was the government offering 'quality services'. Kunshan quickly grasped the opportunity created by the development of Pudong in the early 1990s. With quality services, a warm attitude and an active and efficient approach, Kunshan attracted many FIEs. In terms of business services, Kunshan remade the administrative examination and approval procedures, charged no fee for administrative services, and gave a public commitment regarding administrative examination and approval. This commitment involves: the first office or bureau to handle an enquiry is responsible for providing application materials, and explaining the examination and approval procedures, deadline for application results and charging standards; the government should improve efficiency and complete the examination of the application before the deadline; the government should standardize fees, prohibit additional fees and ensure that fees don't increase. In order to deepen the meaning of contractual services, Kunshan brought out 'three-all' services in a timely manner: all government workers take part in the services, visit and serve enterprises regularly and get to know their requirements; services cover all areas; services such as counseling, early-stage examination and approval, construction, production and operation are provided in a single package.

2) Drawing investment with industrial chains and improving industry support Kunshan worked out its mode of attracting investment with industrial chains when making industrial planning revolve around the upstream and downstream sectors of an industry. One of its modal types is developing from top to bottom: when bringing in an FIE, especially a leading one, Kunshan tracks its upstream and downstream enterprises elsewhere in China, and draws on their industrial connections to attract upstream and downstream enterprises to Kunshan. Another type of mode is developing from bottom to top: recognizing the absence of certain connections in its area, Kunshan introduces enterprises in target areas; it brings in what it lacks to complete its industrial links so as to attract more FIEs, especially transnational ones. Wherever a link is absent in the industrial chain, staff will work to attract enterprises that can fill the link. Such a purpose-oriented mode helped Kunshan quickly optimize its industrial structure and reduce its cost to support enterprises within the zone and thereby greatly increasing Kunshan's appeal to foreign businessmen.

One of the important measures taken by Kunshan in order to enhance its environment to industrial development is 'advance planning': planning as a wealthy man and developing as a poor man. 'Planning as a wealthy man' means looking to the future, making scientific plans and pursuing creative designs, to complete functions, to build supporting facilities and establish high standards. 'Developing as a poor man' means being diligent and thrifty, working hard, discarding ostentation and extravagance, and spending less to get more accomplished. Instead of carrying out 'enclosure campaigns' or attempting to plant flowers everywhere, Kunshan follows the principle of deciding the location and size of the land requisitioned according to the state of infrastructure construction; of developing one area well before proceeding to the next; of doing what it can within its means and of expanding step by step.

3) Boosting independent innovation while opening up Exploration and innovation is the soul of the Kunshan mode, as well as the inexhaustible driving force for securing advantages. Kunshan manufacturing is becoming Kunshan creation. Kunshan's economy is turning from one being driven by resources to one being advanced by talent and innovations. The major measures to realize these transformations are as follows.

Kunshan continuously elevates its innovative urban platform and brings to completion its functions as the carrier of innovation. Kunshan HTDZ is the nation's first of its kind at county-level. Kunshan Photoelectric Industry Park is among the nation's first group of emerging industry demonstration bases and national panel-display high- and new-tech industry bases. Kunshan constantly strengthens its support for the construction of an innovative city and perfects the scientific and technological innovation system. A scientific and technological innovation system that is marked by 'one park, three districts and multiple bases' has started to take shape; it has also built the four platforms – scientific and technological innovation, industrial agglomeration, talent support and sustainable development. Kunshan has built cooperative ties with more than half of the nation's '985' and '211' engineering colleges and universities; it has founded 494 entities that combine production, study and research, 580 research and development institutions of all kinds, four academic workshops, 15 postdoctoral research sites and 21 postdoctoral research site branches.

Kunshan continuously furthers its function as an innovative city and highlights the leading role played by enterprises. In the three years following the 18th National Congress of the CPC, Kunshan has had more than 200 scientific and technological projects listed in national or provincial scientific and technological special plans, undertaken 21 national '863' and '973' planned projects, and received 40,789 patents. Enterprises own 90% of the innovative talent and 90% of the research and development centers, and have contributed 90% of the scientific and technological input and 90% of scientific and technological achievements. Weixinnuo Organic Light Emitting Display Material Project was awarded first prize in the National Award for Technological Invention in 2011.

Kunshan maintains its vitality as an innovative city and brings together top-level innovative talent. It earmarks a special fund for scientific and technological talent, amounting to no less than 6% of the financial budget, pursues a Rmb1m reward policy for talented staff who can meet six different criteria (known as the 'six millions' policy), and strives to bring in and train modern people to construct the new city, core talent to lead new industries, and professional people to serve the new talent. Kunshan boasts 240,000 skilled workers, having introduced 15 academicians from the Chinese Academy of Sciences and the Chinese Academy of Engineering and nine recipients of the Yangtze River scholars award. It has also jointly built a '1,000-talent program workshop' with domestic colleges. So far, 31 people from this program have arrived in Kunshan to innovate or start businesses.

In summary, as far as attracting business and investment is concerned, the environment serves as the base; projects constitute the life; services embody the brand; industries are the pillars; and innovation is the root. As we all know, detecting problems reflects good political performance; addressing problems directly is responsibility; researching problems means progress and solving problems shows ability. The rapid development of Kunshan's economy is closely related to its skilled workers, location and policies, and to its development environment. It's a result of the interaction between Kunshan's inner hard struggle and external environment. We should learn from Kunshan on how to emancipate the mind, grasp opportunities, give full play to individual initiative, stimulate entrepreneurship, be scientifically orientated and sufficiently courageous to tackle prevailing challenges.

6.5 The construction of China (Shanghai) Pilot Free Trade Zone

In August 2013, the State Council officially approved the scheme to establish China (Shanghai) Pilot Free Trade Zone. An FTZ refers to a specific area where a special economic management system and special policies are practiced in foreign economic activities such as cargo supervision, foreign exchange management, tax policies and enterprise establishment. There are many types of FTZ, including free port zones, free economic zones and foreign trade zones. The construction of Shanghai FTZ benefits our nation to forge new global competitive advantages, build new platforms for cooperation with other countries, create new space for economic growth and produce an upgraded version of the Chinese economy.

Shanghai FTZ is a regional special economic zone that is built within the borders of the country (or district) and in line with local laws and regulations. Shanghai FTZ, actually a free trade park, is a small FTZ internationally. It is similar to the 100 or so special customs controlling zones in China. Before the founding of Shanghai FTZ, China had already built six types of special economic zone that are similar to the free trade zone, such as the bonded zone, bonded logistic park and bonded port area. Shanghai FTZ is the first real free trade zone ever built by the state and located inside the territory, but it is exempt from the intervention of customs authorities, in areas such as boundary lines, second-tier control and freedom within the zone. Its functions and high degree of freedom are important attributes for countries worldwide to gather global production factors, participate in the global division of labor and economic competition, and drive economic development. Shanghai FTZ's prominent function and high degree of freedom have already facilitated the following: first, freedom for goods to come in and go out – all goods that conform to internationally accepted practice can enter or leave without any obstruction or regular supervision of customs; second, investment freedom – the nationality of an investment will not affect its operations; third, financial freedom, which mainly includes foreign exchange freedom and freedom in the flow and transfer of funds.

6.5.1 The objectives and functional orientation of China (Shanghai) Free Trade Zone

Shanghai Free Trade Zone is positioned as an 'experimental field' that is designed to push forward reform and encourage an open economy. It adopts special supervisory and preferential tax policies. They are aimed at greatly promoting the nation's shipping and offshore trade.

(1) General objectives After three to five years of effort, Shanghai FTZ will be built into a zone complete with internationally advanced innovations, a fully developed service trade, convenient trade and investment, freedom of currency exchange, flourishing offshore business, efficient and convenient supervision, clustered operational headquarters, a standardized legal environment, and good administrative efficiency and transparency. Shanghai FTZ will then become an important vehicle for China to get deeply involved in the Asia-Pacific economy and integrate it into economic globalization. It will play an exemplary role in upgrading the Chinese economy.

(2) Functional orientation A pilot zone is intended to abide by international investment rules and play a leading role in reforming and upgrading the service trade. It is also intended to be a gathering point for offshore industries; to be a pioneering zone to serve investment from abroad; to be a zone that can lead the optimization of supervisory functions and a demonstration zone to innovate administration.

Shanghai FTZ encompasses four special customs-controlling zones including Shanghai Waigaoqiao FTZ, Waigaoqiao Bonded Logistics Park, Yangshan Free Trade Port Zone and Shanghai Pudong Airport FTZ, with a total area of 28.78 square kilometers (see map below).

Near the estuary of the Yangtze river, at the junction of a golden waterway and a golden coastline, and close to Waigaoqiao port district, Shanghai Waigaoqiao Free Trade Zone covers a planned area of 10 square kilometers, of which 8.9 square kilometers is currently in operation. It is China's first bonded zone, having the largest economy and the best economic performance among all special customs-controlling areas. Waigaoqiao FTZ is China's first bonded zone whose establishment was approved by the State Council in June 1990, with a planned area of 10 square kilometers. After more than 20 years of development, Waigaoqiao FTZ has attracted nearly 10,000 enterprises of all kinds, and has become China's largest special customs controlling area with the most complete business functions. In September 2011, Waigaoqiao FTZ was designated by the Ministry of Commerce as the nation's first 'national innovation demonstration zone for promoting imports', becoming an important international trade base in Shanghai. It expanded and strengthened 10 specialized trade platforms for alcoholic drink, clocks and watches, engineering machinery, machine tools, medical apparatus and instruments, biomedicine, health care products, cosmetics and cultural products. One of these platforms, the cultural trade platform, was named by the Ministry of Culture as the nation's first 'national foreign cultural base'. Waigaoqiao FTZ's scale of specialized commodity trade continued to expand. In 2012, its import of watches, alcohol and cosmetics accounted for 43%, 37% and 29%, respectively, of the national totals; its import of medicines and medical apparatus and instruments increased by 40% and 29% respectively, accounting for 24% and 21% of the national totals.

Adjacent to Waigaoqiao Port Area, covering 1.03 square kilometers, Waigaoqiao Bonded Logistics Park is China's first zone-port bonded logistics park and enjoys both the preferential policies granted to bonded zones and export processing zones and the resources of Shanghai port. In December 2003, the State Council approved the establishment of our nation's first bonded logistic park with a planned area of 1.03 square kilometers.

Yangshan Free Trade Port Area consists of the land part of Shanghai Luchao port, Donghai bridge and Xiaoyangshan port located in Shengsi, Zhejiang province. It is projected to have a planned area of 14.16 square kilometers, with an area of 8.14 square kilometers already in operation. It is being built jointly by Shanghai and Zhejiang and adopts a special supervision by customs. It is our nation's first free trade port area approved by the State Council, in June 2005. It is projected to have a planned area of 14.16 square kilometers and consists of Xiaoyangshan port, and the land area and bridge connecting Xiaoyangshan island with the mainland. As the core functional area for Shanghai's construction of an 'international shipping development comprehensive pilot zone', Yangshan Free Trade Port Area has a distribution and delivery center that deals with communication and electronic products, automobiles and auto parts, luxury food, brand clothing and so on. It has formed a distribution and delivery base aimed at European countries and the US, a staple commodity industrial base, an import trade base aimed at the domestic market, and a gathering place for leading shipping enterprises. It is the fastest growing and generates the most output benefits, including profits, productivity and tax revenue, among all 14 free trade port areas across the nation.

Sitting to the west of the third runway of Pudong airport, adjacent to Yangshan Free Trade Port Area in the south, and with 3.59 square kilometers in operation, Shanghai Pudong Airport FTZ is one of the central nodes in the region along the east coastline of Pudong New District. In July 2009, the State Council approved its establishment. The comprehensive airport FTZ has brought into full play its advantages as a composite hub of Asia Pacific aviation and actively developed a 'pilot innovation area of aviation services'. It is an airborne freight distribution center for many world-famous transnational enterprises, covering fields such as electronic products, medical apparatus and instruments, and luxury consumer goods. It has also brought in hundreds of financial leasing projects. UPS, DHL and FedEx, three of the largest global express companies, have set up bases in the area. With a group of important projects in operation, the comprehensive airport FTZ has gradually formed an aviation service chain, including an Asia Pacific air freight distribution center, financial leasing center, transshipment center, and exhibition space for luxury consumer goods.

6.5.2 The objectives of constructing China (Shanghai) Pilot FTZ

China (Shanghai) Pilot Free Trade Zone is intended to further expand and open up the tertiary industry, push forward the reform of investment management, expedite the exploration of convertibility under the capital account, accelerate the full opening up of the financial services sector, and realize various innovation and reform objectives by drawing on two or three years of experiments and exploration.

Let us first discuss the field of investment. The following three steps have been taken to guarantee the quality of investment. 1) Providing pre-establishment national treatment on a trial basis. On the principle of being consistent with the policy of 'pre-establishment national treatment' concerning both foreign and domestic investment, the zone takes the lead in reforming within the pilot area 'three access links' – access to projects, establishment and change of FIEs, and business registration. 2) Researching and establishing the negative list administrative mode. In accordance with the requirements of developing China's tertiary industry and the functional orientation of the pilot zone, the zone takes the lead in choosing 'six services fields' (finance, shipping, commerce and trade, professions, culture and society), in cancelling qualification requirements and limitations on share proportion and business scope, and in expanding openness both internally and externally. 3) Building a system to improve services to foreign investment. The zone reforms the system to improve investment services, perfects the market operation mechanism, and nourishes a good environment that is beneficial to giving full scope to the enthusiasms and creativity of all investors. The zone reforms the methods of administrating overseas investment, enhances post-investment affairs management, encourages overseas equity investment, supports overseas investment in the form of non-currency assets, and encourages enterprises to adopt the stock-based incentive distribution mechanism in line with international conventions.

Second, let us look at the field of trade. We have done two things to realize our goals. 1) Innovating the development mode of trade. The zone actively cultivates new formats and functions of trade, forms new competitive advantages of foreign trade with technology, brands, quality and services at the core, accelerates the promotion of China's status in the value chain of global trade, facilitates the development of service trade and offshore trade, and brings about the unification of domestic and foreign trade. 2) Innovating policies to promote the development of international shipping. The zone encourages cooperation between Waigaoqiao port, Yangshan deepwater port and Pudong international airport (an international hub), and explores the formation of a competitive shipping development system and operation function.

Third, let us consider the field of finance, where we have taken two concrete measures. 1) Deepening financial reform and innovation. The zone removes the control over capital accounts, marketizes interest rates, fully promotes cross-border use of the renminbi, fully opens financial services to private and foreign capital, allows financial markets to build transaction platforms that face the world, supports the market to come out with their own exchange-traded products, supports banks to organize cross-border transfer and settlement and ecommerce transaction platforms, supports equity exchange institutions to set up comprehensive financial service platforms, supports the start of a cross-border renminbi settlement reinsurance business, cultivates and develops an international insurance market, and builds a linkage mechanism between financial reform and innovation and the construction of Shanghai International Financial Center. 2) Optimizing the foreign exchange policy environment. The zone implements pilot reforms to explore exchange management that faces the world, builds an exchange management system suitable for a pilot free trade zone, makes trade and investment convenient in an all-round way, encourages enterprises to fully utilize domestic and international resources and home and foreign markets so as to liberalize cross-border financing, and deepens the reform of the foreign debt management method to make cross-border financing easy and convenient. This is also done to further the experiment of pooling foreign funds from the headquarters of transnational companies so that a centralized operation and management can be realized and transnational companies are encouraged to set up regional or global fund management centers in Shanghai.

Fourth, let us shift our attention to administrative and legal systems. The zone deepens the reform of the administrative system, expedites the shifting of government functions, modifies government administrative methods and creates a market environment suitable for fair competition. Let us illustrate them in detail. 1) The zone adopts the service mode by which all procedures concerning reception, acceptance and comprehensive examination and approval are to be accomplished through one channel. 2) The zone builds a unified and comprehensive law enforcement system to supervise the market. 3) The zone improves the transparency of government administration. 4) The zone perfects the guarantee system to effectively protect investors' rights and interests. And 5) the zone has installed different settlement mechanisms, such as mediation and assistance to resolve intellectual property rights disputes.

Finally, let us turn to supervision and taxation. Here, we have taken two major measures. 1) Innovation of the supervisory mode. Reforming and optimizing the mechanism and *modus operandi* of customs supervision is the key aim for Shanghai Comprehensive Free Trade Zone to build the pilot FTZ and the precondition for furthering the experiment with opening up trade and investment. The basic objective is to thoroughly open up the frontier step by step, control the second tier safely and efficiently, and allow goods to flow freely within the zone. 2) Supportive tax policies. In order to build Shanghai FTZ into an international center for finance, shipping, trade and culture, preferential tax policies are granted to companies that can help bring about such a development. The zone has started a pilot reform of the tax system, takes the lead to adjust related tax policies, integrates its tax reform into the national tax reform framework and builds a policy environment that facilitates investment and innovation. The basic objective is to make tax policies that can promote investment and trade and match the customs' supervisory mode.

Chapter 6

The construction of Shanghai FTZ accommodates the new development tendencies of global trade and constitutes a significant step, signifying a more aggressive opening-up tactic. The major tasks of Shanghai FTZ are to explore new routes and modes for China to open up, expedite the transformation of government functions, push forward the reform of the administrative system, facilitate a shift in the economic growth mode, retool the economic structure, draw on opening up for further development, reform and innovation, and accumulate more experiences that can be replicated and generalized, and to serve the purpose of developing the whole nation.

The construction of Shanghai FTZ contributes significantly to forging China's fresh international competitive advantages, building new platforms for its cooperation with other nations, expanding space and scope for economic growth and creating an 'upgraded version' of the Chinese economy.

Chapter Follow-up Questions and References

Chapter 1

Questions:

1. What do you think of the planned economic system that China practiced before reform and opening up?
2. Why was China's reform and opening up a choice of history?

References:

1. Wu Jinglian. *A Coursebook on Contemporary Chinese Economic Reform*. Shanghai: Shanghai Yuandong Press, 2010
2. Zou Dongtao. *A Blue Book on Development and Reform — the 30 Years of China's Reform and Opening up (1978-2008)*. Beijing: Social Sciences Academic Press, 2008

Chapter 2

Questions:

1. What method does China's economic system reform adopt? Why?
2. What phases has China's economic system reform undergone? What is the orientation and objective of the reform?

References:

1. Wu, Jinglian. *On the Competitive Market System*. Beijing: Chinese Financial & Economic Publishing House, 1991
2. Wu, Jinglian. *Economic Reform in Contemporary China: Strategies and Practices*. Shanghai: Shanghai Far East Press, 1999
3. Wu, Xiaobo. *Thirty Eventful Years*. Beijing: China Citic Press; Hangzhou: Zhejiang People's Press, 2007

4. Liu, Guoguang. *The New Period of China's Economic Reform and Development*. Beijing: Economic & Management Publishing House, 1996

Chapter 3

Questions:

1. What are the major achievements of China's reform and opening up?
2. What are the characteristics of an economy with mixed ownership? Why does China choose an economy with mixed ownership?

References:

1. Wu Jinglian. *Developing China's High and New Technology Industry: System More Important than Technology*. Beijing: China Development Press, 2002
2. Wu Jinglian and Ma Guochuan. *Restarting the Agenda of Reform: Twenty Articles on China's Economic Reform*. Beijing: SDX Joint Publishing Company, 2013
3. Guo Jianning. *Reform and Opening Up and Socialism with Chinese Characteristics*. Beijing: Peking University Press, 2010
4. Guo Jianning. *Decisions of the Third Plenary Session of the 18th Central Committee of the CPC*. Beijing: People's Publishing House, 2013

Chapter 4

Questions:

1. What reforming ideas are embodied in the important measures of China's economic system reform?
2. What is the basic experience of China's economic system reform? Can other developing countries draw lessons from it, and, if so, how?
3. What important measures has the Chinese government taken to maintain political and social stability?

References:

1. Zhou Qiren. *The Logic of Reform*. Beijing: China Citic Press, 2013
2. Yao Yang. *The Global Meaning of the Chinese Method*. Beijing: Peking University Press, 2011
3. Chang Xiuze. *On the Inclusiveness of Reform: New Thoughts about Comprehensive Reform in the New Period in China*. Beijing: Economic Science Press, 2013

Chapter 5

Questions:

1. What are the practices relating to China's construction of development zones?
2. What are the achievements of the construction of development zones?

References:

1. Li Zhenyuan, and Wu Jilin. *The Theories and Practices Relating to the Construction and Management of Development Zones*. Beijing: People's Publishing House, 2010
2. Li Yaoyao. *The Theory on Agglomeration Development: Considering the Evolution of China's Development Zones from the Perspective of Economics*. Guangzhou: Jinan University Press, 2011

Chapter 6

Questions:

1. What is the successful experience of the construction of Shenzhen SEZ?
2. What are the achievements related to the development and opening up of Pudong, Shanghai?

References:

1. Tang Minggen. *Engine: Mission of the Age of China's Development Zones*. Beijing: Economic Press China, 2010
2. Li Sen. *The Predicament and the Way out – Research on the Development of China's Development Zones During the Transitional Period*. Beijing: Chinese Financial and Economic Publishing House, 2008